Exotic Brew

Adolph von Menzel, *Tavola rotunda*. Frederick II of Prussia banqueting with Voltaire at the Sans-Souci palace, 1850. Oil on wood, 204 × 175 cm. © Nationalgalerie, Berlin. Photograph: Archiv fur Kunst und Geschichte, Berlin.

EXOTIC BREW

The Art of Living in the Age of Enlightenment

Piero Camporesi

Translated by Christopher Woodall

POLITY PRESS

Copyright © Garzanti Editore SpA, 1990. First published as *Il Brodo Indiano*
This English translation © Polity Press 1994
First published in 1994 by Polity Press in association with Blackwell Publishers Ltd
First published in paperback 1998

Editorial office:
Polity Press, 65 Bridge Street
Cambridge CB2 1UR, UK

Marketing and production:
Blackwell Publishers Ltd, 108 Cowley Road
Oxford OX4 1JF, UK

Published in the USA by
Blackwell Publishers Inc., 350 Main Street
Malden MA 02148, USA

All rights reserved. Except for the quotation of short passages for the purposes of criticism and review, no part of this publication may be reproduced, stored in a retrieval system, or transmitted, in any form or by any means, electronic, mechanical, photocopying, recording or otherwise, without the prior permission of the publisher.

Except in the United States of America, this book is sold subject to the condition that it shall not, by way of trade or otherwise, be lent, re-sold, hired out, or otherwise circulated without the publisher's prior consent in any form of binding or cover other than that in which it is published and without a similar condition including this condition being imposed on the subsequent purchaser.

A CIP catalogue record for this book is available from the British Library.

Library of Congress Cataloging-in-Publication Data
Camporesi, Piero.
    [Brodo Indiano. English]
    Exotic brew : the art of living in the age of enlightenment /
Piero Camporesi.
    p. cm.
    Translation of : Il Brodo Indiano.
    Includes bibliographical references and index.
    ISBN 0–7456–0877–9   ISBN 0–7456–2197–X (pbk.)
    1. Food habits—Italy—History—18th century. 2. Food habits—Europe—History—18th century. 3. Diet—Italy—History—18th century. 4. Diet—Europe—History—18th century. I. Title.
GT2853.I8C3513   1994
392.1'0945'09033—dc20   94–27800
                                                            CIP

Typeset in 11 on 13 pt Bembo by Best-set Typesetter Ltd, Hong Kong
Printed in Great Britain by TJ International, Padstow, Cornwall
This book is printed on acid-free paper.

CONTENTS

1	THE SCIENCE OF *SAVOIR VIVRE*	1
2	THE REVENGE OF THE NIGHT	12
3	GOOD COOKS AND SKILFUL HAIRDRESSERS	27
4	THE PURGED CENTURY	36
5	HEAVY AND VISCOUS MEATS	46
6	THE STRANGE NEW ADOPTIONS OF LISTLESS GLUTTONY	54
7	EPHEMERAL DÉCOR	64
8	A BLISSFUL AND DRINKABLE ETERNITY	72
9	THE BOTANY OF THE PALATE	83
10	PERFIDIOUS ART	96
11	INDIAN BROTH	108
12	MAD AND STARTLING NAMES	122
13	QUINTESSENCES OF JUICES	129
14	THE LAVISH TABLE	138
	Notes	161
	Index	184

ONE

THE SCIENCE OF *SAVOIR VIVRE*

The crisis in European consciousness that Paul Hazard situates between 1680 and 1715 coincided with a revolution in the tradition of late-Renaissance eating and dining arts and the gradual distancing of Italy from the centres of cultural innovation. These 'harsh packed years, full of struggles and upheavals and brimming with thought' saw the cultural axis shift from central-southern Europe to the north-west, from the Mediterranean to the North Sea. Over the next two centuries the grammar of European cuisine would follow patterns quite different from those of the Roman–Florentine school: the light now flooding from Versailles was to penetrate even Italy's refined Renaissance courts.

Along with the gospels of the *nouveaux philosophes*, the France of the *conquérants*, of the warmongering, quick-tempered Gauls, began to export armies of cooks and *coiffeurs*, tailors and dancing masters, empiricist popularizers and social interpreters of the newest trends to emerge from its burgeoning *civilisation*. With that tinge of cloying, inverted provincialism which was as irritating then as it is now, Pietro Verri complained that the 'science of *savoir vivre*' and 'certain social delicacies, which the French understand so well, are quite unknown to us Italians, especially in the southern part of Italy'.[1]

Many a noble cuisine fell into the hands of Frenchifying cooks who proceeded with lofty pigheadedness to enforce the new laws of their transalpine code. Giuseppe Parini watched them with ill-concealed irritation and poked fun at the pompous theatricality that accompanied the exploits of these new *maîtres* who, from their 'lowliest workshops', sought to prepare for the noble palates 'a harsh tickling' that would 'shake up softened nerves / and carry with it a varied voluptuousness'.[2]

> In white garments
> valiant ministers hurry to perform
> the noble task: and their laws are dictated by
> a great mind, issuing from the country
> where Colbert and Richelieu were once renowned...
>   Oh thou, wise master
> of palatal flattery, soon shall thou hear
> thy praises sounding from that elevated table.
> Whoever would dare to find even a blemish
> in thy work?[3]

The 'first cook expressly brought from Paris', the 'French first official of cookery' (as the Bolognese playwright Marquis Francesco Albergati Capacelli called him in his *Lettere capricciose*), became a central character, a revered dignitary, entrusted with the fine-tuning of that complex machinery designed to deliver, at any hour or minute of the nobility's lengthy day, tasty little titbits for difficult and jaded tastebuds.

Not everyone was willing, however, to acknowledge the pre-eminent and trail-blazing role that France had played in the honing of manners and the refinement of lifestyles. Count Francesco Algarotti, a great and distinguished traveller who was as much at home in Paris as in Berlin, in St Petersburg as in London, a dining companion in Potsdam of Frederick II and of Voltaire, certainly entertained doubts. In a letter written in 1752 to Carlo Innocenzo Frugoni, a poet of the Bourbon court in Parma, Algarotti pointed out that

> in the delicacies of life, where there are so many Absolute Masters, the French have no choice but to acknowledge their teachers. Montaigne in one of his *Essays* mentions a servant employed by Cardinal Caraffa as a meat carver, who was a great expert in the

science of culinary dainties, sauces and every other means of reviving even the most spoiled and erudite of appetites. This carver well knew

> *Quo gestu lepores, et quo gallina secetur.*
> [With what gesture to chop a hare or a hen.]

Elsewhere, Montaigne reports that in his time the French would go to Italy to learn dancing, high fashion and genteel manners, just as the English now come to us to study the work of Palladio and to pore over the remains of ancient buildings. So when the French speak ill of us, one might well say, to borrow one of their own expressions, the child is striking out at its own wetnurse.

The fact is that after Europe's shared period of barbarism, the Italians opened their eyes before all other nations. When the others were still sleeping, we were wide awake.[4]

The process of modernization which Italy had launched had been so intense that it now seemed that dark age 'barbarism', expelled at last by the 'enlighteners', had rendered the country quite unrecognizable. In Saverio Bettinelli's fantasy the fourteenth-century poet Petrarch, returning to the Italian peninsula from the Kingdom of Shadows after an absence of 'more than four centuries'[5] spent in the company of Love, was disconcerted by the unimaginable and 'strange confusion' that greeted him. Everything had changed since the time when 'all was Gothic, that is to say German'.[6] Bettinelli's description went to extremes that were grotesque and unexpected, especially in that 'century of things',[7] a time when geometrical formulae were pressed into service to explain even the mysteries of the hereafter and when 'sermons were composed, if not actually pronounced, using words and theorems derived from Wolf's mathematical method'.[8] So, plummeting from heaven to earth, catapulted from his 'rough age' into a world that had been transformed beyond recognition, Petrarch's ghost was dumbfounded by all the 'wondrous progress' that paraded before his dazed traveller's eyes.[9] 'Speech, dress, lodgings, conversation, home life, arts and crafts, laws, customs, religion itself: how different it all is from before,' the poet remarked.[10]

Looking round him, he could see an open and pleasant urban landscape where, instead of 'castles and towers' and 'battlements and parapets' built by fierce and mighty men living in their manors like lions in their dens and 'shut up, nay buried, even in their cities', there soared slender, elegant 'palaces decorated with gold, with stucco, with paintings, complete with doors and marble halls, broad façades and large glass windows reaching right down to the ground and making the long sweep of rooms all the brighter and more beautiful'.[11]

Bright, well-lit suites of airy rooms with gold-decorated ceilings and large, sinuous windows: this comfortable and civilized new architecture emphasized the break with the Gothic past, racked as it had been by fears, phantoms, gloomy visions, blood-spattered traps and miscellaneous 'horrors'. Petrarch was particularly fascinated by luxurious and spacious eighteenth-century stairs, which he considered 'magnificent' and utterly different from the 'dark and narrow' stairs that he had known in his days. Interiors struck him as so inviting and elegant that he cried out in admiration:

> And that furniture, the luxury of those broad, soft chairs, those carpeted and canopied beds, those walls hung with fine fabrics, the crockery so costly and glittering! Some pieces, said to be porcelain, I was afraid even to touch. It all seemed to me a dream and an enchantment.[12]

The most refined luxury went hand in hand with an inimitable and exquisite fashion:

> their clothes also are of the highest elegance, clinging to their limbs so that they do not appear covered, their heads all powdered and protected by three-pointed ridged felt hats, their necks close-swathed; and yet so slight and scanty is such apparel that they can dance at any moment, their legs visible and disencumbered, their dainty feet in sparkling golden buckles with fine gems like those that we would have used to ornament our hands.[13]

There had also been far-reaching changes in the general economy of meals, in the various courses and in the taste of the food itself. Less sumptuous than the dining-tables of the newly rich, whose wealth indeed was amassed by illicitly tapping into the customs revenues of the princes, and who were creatures of such 'contemptible manners' that they would make the 'publicans of old' appear like strict 'stoics',[14] the tables of the nobility were embellished not, of course, by the 'plebeian exultation' proper to the petty-bourgeois revels of ill-bred upstarts but by 'exquisite foods and foreign wines, of which each diner had a catalogue, the better to select whatever seemed to him to be best'. Vanished from noble tables was that barbaric jumble and chaotic parading of gigantic courses that had characterized the medieval meal, those 'huge dishes of my days', as Petrarch commented, 'top-heavy with game or with fowl heaped in pyramids or with whole calves and kids'.[15]

The heavy curtain of spices whose dense and memory-numbing smells encircled the medieval banquet had vanished into thin air, along with the rose water once used in preprandial baths.

> Nothing any longer smells of those spices that were then so rare and that we so appreciated in every dish. Nor does one now see dinner-tables bearing either those immense cakes or those towering pastries or those jets of rose or jasmine water. Little food but in many courses, in precious sauces, rich extracts and thick gravies. The only thing that struck me amidst such luxury was that no one washed their hands before the meal.[16]

To wash one's hands before dining would be 'to confess that one was dirty', Love explains to Petrarch in the *Dialoghi*, 'which is something that must not even be suspected in persons who are so elegant from head to foot'.[17] The new elegance, a luxury that was both delicate and exquisite, a sinuous fashion of clinging clothes, designed – one might think – to emphasize the body's lightness and agility, demanded a novel style in food and a different status for cooking.

Little food but lots of courses: a subtle palette of tastes orchestrated to underscore their variety and to enhance the play of flavours that overlapped and contrasted but must not amalgamate. It was a highly-strung and agile syntax of cookery, far removed from the ancient cuisine where rough-and-ready abundance crushed the sensitive and yielding palate under a cascade of 'immense cakes' and 'towering pastries'.

Vanished now were those patriarchal courses that had seen large game and the meat of heavy and solid quadrupeds led past in oily procession only to slither from their enormous trays on to the broad chopping-boards and thence into the capacious plates of the dinner guests. In their place, modern culinary art now struggled to produce a fashion show of minute, winnowy and fragile crockery on which were presented 'precious sauces', 'extracts and thick gravies', consommés and thick broths, purées and gelatines, the cooks' alchemical skill being employed to extract the spirit of the flesh from the vulgar ruddy hunks of dead meat in which it dwelled. The resulting fare discharged the fine *mangeurs* from the trivial need to bite, to tear and to munch, thereby freeing them to engage in elegant discussions and lively conversations.

Eighteenth-century dining-tables were dominated by a new *ratio convivalis* (way of setting up a feast), a geometrical order and a mathematical reason: the multiplicity of the dishes presupposed the lightness of the substances on offer and the variety of tastes was bodied forth in their shimmering colours. The eye, by dethroning the nose, had enhanced the colourfulness of the parade, the brilliance of the cups' minuet and the victuals' dance. Polychromy and miniaturization fused in the meal's well-tempered concert as in an elegant musical phrase. What dominated was the overarching apparatus, the *order* and the harmonic discipline that presided over the carefully thought out procession of dishes, or rather over their visually appetizing and multicoloured *promenade*, produced and directed for the finicky pleasure of sight. The eye became the cutting edge of the most subtle of tastes, a sensitive device empowered to provide from a distance both a measurement and a morphological assessment. The eye, that least confiding and least carefree of the senses, that icy, impassive director, could miss no detail as it strolled and slithered and strayed across the highly coloured surfaces without exploring the *intérieur*, without scenting or touching the hidden soul of the substances themselves.

Already the table is being laid. In a thousand
guises, a thousand flavours, a thousand colours
the varied legacy of our ancestors
makes merry in the dishes; and retains just measure.[18]

For the benefit of Italian noblewomen, Francesco Algarotti had invented 'a new kind of pleasure', transplanting from France 'the fashion of cultivating one's mind rather than a new way of curling one's hair',[19] thereby considerably enriching this 'century of things and of universal culture'.[20] Indeed, the new 'purged century' had relegated to the level of dusty and dangerous old junk not only 'stale Gothic lumber', 'rancid old words',[21] magic exoticism, pre-scientific animism and the culture of the schools, but also the disorder and muddled excess of medieval, Renaissance and baroque dining-tables. The mathematics of the spirit, the 'doctrine of measures and the infallible science of numerical quantities', had brought about a fundamental change in direction, an absolute U-turn, even as regards food itself. The dinner-table was becoming the condensation chamber for the new frontiers of the mind, the board on which a game was played entailing the reconversion of human nature to the rules of reason and science. 'Might not taste be defined,' asked Algarotti in his 'Pensieri diversi', 'as the doctrine of proportions applied to the geometry of the spirit?'[22]

This 'geometry of the spirit' was, however, more often the object of theory than the stuff of everyday life and experience. Indeed, it was not rare for *philosophes*, when they met at table, to forget all about the 'doctrine of proportions' and to abandon themselves to pre-scientific excesses, to lavish revels, worthy of those rough and sombre centuries, of those ancient obscurantist and superstitiously deviant diets, so deleterious and lethal for any supple and light spirit that had ever laughed to scorn the barbaric ways and deplorable customs of Gothic medieval society. From his vantage point in Naples, as he mulled over the Fridays he had spent in Paris, Abbot Ferdinando Galiani, who, unlike other Enlightenment thinkers, continued to abstain from meat on that day of the week, harked back with nostalgia to the bouts of fish-induced indigestion that his solid appetite had then caused him. 'Dinner would be announced. We would go out, the others ate rich meats while I confined myself to fish. I would eat a lot of that green Scottish hake that I like so much, and it would give me indigestion, while I sat admiring Abbot Morellet's skill in carving a pullet. We would rise from the table, take coffee and everyone would talk at once.'[23]

The meals of Enlightenment philosophers almost always ended with indigestion, even those of 'that rare spirit, Monsieur de Voltaire', who could still somehow manage to make an evening extraordinary and unforgettable. Count Algarotti, chamberlain to Frederick the Great and thus a frequent dining companion of Voltaire at Frederick's table, recalled that 'a dinner without Voltaire seemed almost like a ring without a gem'.

Algarotti wrote that at the Sans-Souci palace, during the 'King's dinners', 'thoughts spray from his mouth, alive and sparkling, as sparks and flakes of light from bodies made electric from an excess of rubbing'.[24] Such dinners demanded not only powerful minds but also robust appetites and voracious bellies, foes of abstinence and fasting, enemies to such regular table disciplines as were only fit for people of restricted 'virtues'. As Algarotti, one of Frederick's guests, recounted in 1750 to Francesco Maria Zanotti:

> The greatest virtue is required at these tables. You are almost always presented with wicked dishes, that is to say with just those dishes that make you eat even when you have no appetite at all.
>
> *Hélas! Les indigestions*
> *Sont pour la bonne compagnie.*
>
> I should like to see Luigi Cornaro and his whole treatise on the sober life subjected to such trials.[25]

From Potsdam to the 'Delights' of Geneva, the dietary programme remained essentially (and perilously) the same. 'More spirit than body',[26] extremely thin, 'with a great big black velvet beret over his eyes and beneath that a thick wig framing his face, from which jutted forth a nose and a chin considerably more pointed than in his portraits, his body covered in fur from top to toe',[27] Voltaire purged himself regularly before sitting down to table in order that he could eat his fill without any fear of indigestion. Saverio Bettinelli, who visited Ferney when Voltaire was already over sixty, recalled:

> We lunched in good company and I saw his method of taking a good spoonful of cassia preserve before sitting down to eat and then eating very heartily. After the meal, he said to me: 'I have eaten too much, I shall not live long to enjoy my new house [at Ornex, built, as he used to say, so that he might "go and digest from one place to another"]; but must have pleasure, I am greedy. Horace was too; everyone pursues pleasure. *Il faut bercer l'enfant jusqu'à ce qu'il s'endorme.*'
> As you can see, he belonged to Horace and Epicurus' flock, as he did also to that of Diogenes'; and sometimes he played the part of Socrates and sometimes that of Aristippus. Then, once he had enjoyed several fine bottles, he would drink lots of coffee.[28]

Voltaire's personal doctor, the renowned Tronchin to whom the philosopher had entrusted his 'life and health',[29] 'was not happy with his patient'.[30] This fashionable physician, 'a handsome and gracious man', was fought over by all the 'convulsionaries' who flocked to Geneva from as far away as Paris in order to be examined by him. Tsarina Catherine even offered him a princely contract if he would only abandon the little Calvinist republic on the shore of Lake Leman and move to her palace in St Petersburg. Tronchin's patients were all women of high society with particularly sensitive nerves and delicate wombs, who suffered from the illness that at that time was most widespread among women, convulsionary fits. To these ladies Tronchin offered a 'gallant treatment': 'side-saddle horse-riding each morning, refined lunches and dinners following the method prescribed, gaming tables, flirtation and music by turns, in a word, unceasing fun and games far from their husbands and far from the court'.[31] Thomas Sydenham, known as the 'English Hippocrates', advised patients who presented the same syndrome to read *Don Quixote* and to go riding because 'the horse is the hypochondriac's quinquina'.[32]

Advised and attended by such a doctor, even a difficult patient like Voltaire managed to attain the age of eighty-four without serious mishap. Pleasure without excess, controlled voluptuousness, prudent moderation, noncommittal flirtatiousness and elegant diets.

Yet if the great Tronchin, to whom the Tsarina had offered '60,000 francs a year, a table to share with all his friends, a carriage, house and a gift upon his eventual departure if only he would agree to live at court for three years',[33] prescribed games, music and horse-riding interspersed with 'refined lunches and dinners'[34] for ladies subject to the storms and swoons that went with easy living, libertine seducers, for their part, were in the habit of offering their lovers 'a delicious and excellent dinner, albeit frugal and moderate in quantity'.[35] It took a visionary like De Sade, worthy of Heliogabalus, to conjure up immoderate banquets of a kind quite alien to eighteenth-century good taste and featuring huge mounds of meat and eccentric *simplegma* (intricately structured garnishes) overflowing from dishes piled high.

> First of all there was a soup made with fish stock and twenty dishes of hors-d'œuvres. These were followed by twenty entrées which in their turn gave way to twenty other fine entrées, consisting solely of chicken breasts and game disguised in every possible manner. This was replaced by a course of roast meats that featured everything imaginable that is most rare. After this arrived cold patisserie, which soon yielded to twenty-six sweets of every shape and form. The table was then cleared and what had been removed was replaced by a full spread of cold and hot sugared patisserie. At last the desserts were brought on, comprising a prodigious number of fruits, despite the season, ice-creams, chocolate and liqueurs, the latter to be drunk at the table. As for wines, they were changed at each new course: to start with, burgundy; to accompany the second and third courses, two different types of wine from Italy; for the fourth course, a Rhine wine; for the fifth, some wines from the Rhône valley; for the sixth, sparkling champagne and two kinds of Greek wine.[36]

Yet any gentleman of quality (even if possessed by satyric demons) would have been hard pressed to approve of such a menu conjured up by the perverted taste of the aristocratic prisoner of the Bastille who, in the throes of his diabetic-cum-sexual fits, dreamed of committing *outrances* unacceptable not only to every honest man with an educated palate but even to professional libertines. For a true gentleman, depravity in taste always went hand in hand with licence in manners: an abominable stew and a shameful love affair were one and the same thing; both were associated with a single and harmful principle of corruption. The court too swarmed with 'unoccupied and lazy spirits', with 'tireless and very tiring talkers', with 'scoffing bores',[37] all of whom were 'men of bad taste, of a singular and strange taste, as depraved in their love affairs as in their stews'.[38]

TWO

THE REVENGE OF THE NIGHT

Charles Louis de Secondat, Baron of La Brède and of Montesquieu, once remarked that 'often the husband's day began where his wife's ended'.[1] Eighteenth-century society and 'enlightened' women in particular had overcome the long tyranny of darkness. The poet Parini referred to the 'terrible shadow' that night cast in former days and to 'the horribly silent and opaque air' that blazed with 'great light and with gold'. Meeting in the 'superb hall', the 'nocturnal council' glowed in the light of 'hundreds of torches'. The 'enemy darkness', reconsecrated by the 'geniuses, / who romp triumphant in the night', would flee from the 'new light', seeking refuge in the heart of the gloomy countryside. Yet in the 'happy recesses' of the 'great palace', all was 'joyousness and light'.

> In amazement, the night sees around her,
> shining more than beneath the sun,
> golden cornices, walls with mirrors
> and crystal hung, sundry finery, white
> shoulders and arms, and darting eyes.
> (Parini, 'La Notte', lines 48–52)

It was during nights lit by glittering chandeliers that the magic power of feminine seduction was at its height. 'Beautiful women,' remarked Pietro Verri, 'prefer to appear at night than during daylight. During the day the great body of light issues from one angle only, all the prominences on the face, all its cavities, assume shadows that make the features stand out. Whereas an admirably lit ballroom receives light from all directions at once; the whole silhouette is thus uniformly lit and almost always bright.'[2]

The 'victory over the night' (F. Braudel) won by 'lamp-women', as Abbot Roberti termed them, had renewed vital rhythms, upset the traditional passage of the hours, profoundly altered the way that people managed their time, undermined age-old customs and dispelled archaic and superstitious fears.

A stealthy, silent revolution was engulfing the old order. The 'sentiment de la nuit' (which Montesquieu wrote about in his 'Essai sur le goût'),[3] an adversary that was impalpable and invisible, but no less tough and insidious for all that, had been permanently defeated and chased out. This 'feeling of the night' bordered on the sinister notion of non-existence, of negative, inert and funereal time, the time of spiritual absence, the empty incubator of death. This lifting of the taboo of the night, the replacement of natural time by cultural time and the new power that art had achieved over nature marked a deep *coupure* in the network of conditioning that had been woven silently over centuries and millennia.

Night-time had lost its sickly aura of sinister hours beloved of witches and sorcerers, the horror of spectral apparitions and the 'noises' of ghosts. Even the quite sensible ban imposed by old-style medicine on the deleterious practice of 'going out at night' and of nocturnal travel – deemed to upset and undermine not only the natural order but the moral one too – had collapsed under the glare of gallant soirées. In the mid sixteenth century Monsignor Sabba Castiglione, among others, warned:

> Except in extreme necessity, take care not to go out at night: first of all, because of the scandals, troubles and dangers that continually ensue; further, because of the diverse and numerous illnesses that night air is wont to generate in human bodies, remembering that the day was made for working and the night for resting; and it is certain that going out at night without need is merely to disturb the order of nature.[4]

To the eyes of the Catholic conservatives of the second half of the eighteenth century, the 'idle and soft' life of the 'disordered century',[5] the corrupted mores of the 'effeminate century',[6] seemed to be the negation of the old civil order and the triumph of dissoluteness, licentiousness and depravity. It was a form of delirium for such a 'crazed century', 'puffed up by a vain science', to claim that it was 'bringing light and happiness to the earth'.[7] It was at night that the 'dissipation of thoughts, the softness of delights . . . where all is trifles and bagatelles, pomp and affectation, idleness and raving',[8] most easily led people to forget the routines of the day and the duties of Christian life bathed in the sunshine of faith rather than in the false glimmers of atheism, deism, Pyrrhonism and atomism. These, by reducing man to 'a pinch of vehemently shaken fine dust' and thought to a chance cluster of pulverized substance that could appear 'triangular or square . . . hard or soft',[9] had finished by proclaiming that men were nothing more than 'machines, that work like clocks'.[10] It was in the heart of the enlightened night that were born the 'putrid sophisms'[11] of the *philosophes*, of the wicked Franco-Dutch masters, of the 'overweening libertines',[12] of the 'free thinkers', the monstrous offspring of the 'oracle of the libertines', of an 'impious Spinoza',[13] of the perfidious glorifiers of 'brutal appetites',[14] of those who were happy to exort others to 'abandon themselves without restraint or proportion into the arms of every wickedness,' 'to enslave themselves to wine, to bed and to food', to 'trample on every right and every law', to 'course like greyhounds over every field sniffing out a filthy and contemptible scrap of enjoyment'.[15] Even in the cities and among those who had remained fundamentally tied to the Catholic tradition and to the old order 'people stay up so much later and longer that they then have to restore themselves by resting until very late the next day. The fact is that they accordingly rise from bed at a time when the celebration of the divine mysteries is almost completely over. The fact is that by the time their hair has been curled, their foreheads polished, their eyes brightened, their cheeks painted, their necklaces arrayed, their ribbons unfurled, their entire demeanour embellished, if it is not yet time for the table to be spread, it is already the time when all the churches are closing.'¹⁶

'Wicked modern customs' had penetrated not just 'conspicuous families' and the 'noble and refined orders'. The 'populace', 'tradesfolk' and all the 'work-shy'[17] would crowd into city taverns, especially on feast days, and stay out late 'to profane the night either at long theatre shows or at continual debauches or in other bouts of utter dissoluteness'.[18] This kind of mistaken, nay perverted, use of the hours of the day afforded the clearest evidence of moral and social disorder,[19] the up-ending of time itself being the clearest indication of an overturning in values:

> Oh mighty and wretched fashion
> that nature's entire order
> overthrows, where only reason
> and sombre faith now reign![20]

Darkness had descended over reason, illuminated only by satanic reflections and a depraved and dissembling madness now smuggled in immoral and dissolute trends. Woman was the engine, inspiration and the ever busy agent of disorder:

> This kind of life,
> wastes and murders health;
> yet is it liked by all,
> who wallow at night only:
> and women are especially
> happy to stay up all night.
>
> May the tainted night air
> make them yellow and ugly:
> yet will our harlots well know
> to appear in the light of the day,
> their faces whitened, lips reddened
> with white lead and with vermilion.[21]

Religious circles and Catholic intellectuals were firmly convinced that society had reached a crucial turning-point, that the 'century of luxury'[22] was fast approaching a break with the traditions, principles and mores of the past, and that a radical change and an unprecedented upheaval were now imminent. The upside-down world was coming soon. This 'strange metamorphosis' would change the very image of humankind. The Carmelite friar Pier Luigi Grossi (1741–1812) remembered the changes in the following terms:

> I think that our century . . . is nothing but an inversion, an overturning of the centuries that preceded us: for in our day rough austerity has been replaced by a seductive culture; bloody ferocity by soft effeminacy; ignorant credulity by philosophical unbelief . . . This change of scenery, this upheaval among minor people, has only lasted a few decades and indeed most of us have been as dumbfounded onlookers before the spectacle. Certain survivors from ancient former times still measure out our land with geometric pace, turning themselves, by their clothing and their features, into the superstitious flaunters of the rusticity of their era; all day long, sullen and severe, they fire untimely invective at today's elegant costumes and at the seductive witchcraft of our sophisticated manners. Therefore shall I spend no further words or time in illustrating to you the strange metamorphosis that has in our days been witnessed in civil society.[23]

The 'strange metamorphosis' that had overtaken the 'ill-omened century'[24] was on display for all to see. Indeed, the 'modern depravities' of 'today's refined good taste',[25] the 'overwhelming dominant culture of dress and manners', the 'excessive culture . . . and this immoderate and profuse parading of clothes', the 'spell-binding eyes and bewitching hearts' of the 'vain and pompous' women and of the 'men decked out with wholly feminine pomp', the 'close tailoring', the 'tight stitching', the 'abject nudity'[26] and the 'lavishness of clothing': such excesses had buried every last vestige of 'Christian moderation'.

'Soft effeminacy',[27] 'interminable series of modern womanly flourishes', 'most lascivious impudence', 'all too oft repeated night-time visits', 'liberty and licence of loose talk', 'modern mincing effeminacy', the 'charm of cajolery', women's enchanting 'vivacity of spirit', 'certain panted courtesies and languorous affectations unceasingly lavished between people of different sex', 'sweet features', 'gracious attentions exchanged in civil company', 'over-elaborate pining and moping', the 'longing and sighing' that 'foment the dangerous commerce of worldly friendships', the 'greedy lust of a voluptuous heart',[28] the 'dominant nonchalance, that would be more accurately termed licence or libertinage';[29] everything served to promote feelings of regretting and sympathy for jealousy, even if it was a 'detestable passion'.[30]

Many people who were attached to tradition had watched in amazement as 'the scenery had suddenly changed'.[31] The 'mixing up' and the 'confusion of the sexes'[32] seemed to have overturned even the classical images of masculinity and femininity. Casting off all modesty, women had lengthened and lightened their figures. In the eyes of Petrarch's ghost, they

> built too high and over-curled their hair, sprinkling it with powder to make it all of a colour, decorating it with an infinity of flowers, leaves, grasses, feathers, veils, ribbons and headbands. They paint their cheeks, flicker their eyes, raise their voices, seeming to me to make themselves men, just as the men by dressing with such gaiety and affectation make themselves women . . . Nothing surprised me more than the freedom of the wives, even to the point of having a deputy-husband always at their sides, the husbands demanding this by law, as if they would be committing a grave fault by remaining by the side of their women.[33]

A new generation of women-flowers had sprung up, light-headed flibbertigibbets, as supple as reeds, as skittish as moths, yet with voices both firm and sure. Lightness was in the air.

Even male fashion seemed to be adopting a feminine taste:

> for their clothes also are of the highest elegance, clinging to their limbs so that they do not appear covered, their heads all powdered and protected by three-pointed ridged felt hats, their necks close-swathed; and yet so slight and scanty is such apparel that they can dance at any moment, their legs visible and disencumbered, their dainty feet in sparkling golden buckles with fine gems.[34]

The new rituals had, however, been adopted by cultivated, wealthy, aristocratic society everywhere. On the eve of the French Revolution *La Toletta*, an elegant pamphlet on weddings, was published in Bologna, with the eminently authoritative endorsement of the city's Institute of Sciences. Written, as was traditional, by several different authors (some of whom were famous and distinguished), it was in effect a collective hymn to the elaborate ceremonies involved in the construction of the feminine idol and to the entertaining game that consisted in leering at the new Venus as she processed along the tortuous paths of a 'modern' day, from the morning hours spent in her 'toletta' gown, via her readings, her 'luminaries' and her 'visits'. The 'negligée' emphasized her hidden beauty while revealing the most pleasing nakedness.

> Oh how can one express
> The charms of such limbs
> When the skirts themselves
> Reveal them so fully!
>
> The way she does not hide
> From every furtive glance
> The warm and living ivory
> Of her palpitating breast!
>
> The way she shows a portion
> Of her elegant and long,
> Snow-white leg so lithe
> And her tiny gracious toe!
>
> With her foot, also adorned,
> With azure silks, there darts
> Into the twining dance
> The messenger of April.[35]

All the instruments and the topoi of eighteenth-century gallant beauty had their eulogists in this choral *toletta*: 'quality of dress', 'dressing-room', 'negligée', 'comb', 'mirror', '*toupet* and curls', 'hairpins', 'cream', 'facepowder', 'bonnet and veils', 'feathers', 'ribbons', 'beauty spots', 'perfumes', 'chocolate', 'books', 'visits', 'luminaries' and 'good taste'.

'The face of the civilized world had changed': 'the barbarism of past centuries had been rebuffed'[36] by a 'suave chain of mutual offices . . . by seductive cultivation in clothing and in features'.[37] But fickle fashion and the 'genius of commerce' had shifted routes and diverted trade while Anglomania and Francomania, by ushering in pointless and costly imports, had impoverished and almost brought to their knees the old and glorious manufactures of the ancient Italian states. The Venetian economy was at last gasp:

> Even our arts, kind Sir, are stolen
> By the hand of foreigners, which love
> Makes cleverer than lucre. The dense
> Scarlet cloth, full coloured and soft
> Of thread, is now woven by strange shuttles;
> And an alien furnace now tempers and fires
> The once noble glasswork of Murano,
> Dear to the Graces and to Chloe, a bright device
> And Honour of the toilet.[38]

Female 'toletta', its mirrors reflecting with morbid tenacity the faces of the 'women of quality', had become the magic fetish of a society that was waking up to its own gallantry – even among its city masses, even among its men. From across the English Channel there arrived 'the fine English fan', the very height of fashion, depicting stories of paladins rather than the customary Chinese landscapes ('here you see no dragons and pagodas / Painted in Peking by a barbarous brush').[39] Fans that were held in the hands of ladies, depending on the rhythm with which they were waved, reflected in turn the various changing passions of the lady who clutched them. As Magalotti wrote to Tommaso Bonaventuri on 10 April 1710:

> if I just see a fan in the hand of a well-disciplined lady, I flatter myself that I can tell at once, without seeing her face, whether she is laughing, blushing or sulking. I have on occasion seen fans so

enraged that I feared for what might become of the gallants who had provoked them should they have the ill fortune to come within reach. And, at the opposite extreme, I have on occasion seen fans waved with such languor and longing that my heart leaped with love for the lady, while her gallant stayed far away from her to avoid falling into a swoon. I think this suffices to demonstrate that a fan can signify wisdom or coquetry according to the temperament of its owner.[40]

From the other side of the Alps, France poured out torrents of lace trimmings, trinketry and millinery.

> By mud-caked coach there reached us yesterday
> She whose arrival has been so eagerly awaited,
> The belle of Paris, the puppet spirit
> Who from every villa raises a flock
> Of 'gentle ladies to love devoted'.
> You might see them before her in droves
> Anatomizing piece by piece her *andrienne*,
> Her headgear, ribbons and her immense
> Crinoline, and pressing their greedy gazes
> Even into and under her petticoats.
> And a very long sleeve this year conceals
> A certain envious part of her arm;
> But a new mitten dare not hide
> That other part for, transparent and black,
> It veils yet enhances her submissive innocence.[41]

On the tables of the nobility, where 'foreign wines / born to slake noble thirsts' sparkled in glasses, from Holland there now arrived the finest of fabrics:

> on the tables
> there glistens
> the finest
> white linen
> that hardy
> Dutch helmsmen
> carry over the waves
> to adorn our grand banquets.[42]

The penchant of the better-off classes for all things foreign harmonized well with the 'impudence of economist-philosophers' who maintained that 'flirtatious women who pursue fashion are much more useful to society than do-gooding Christian ones'.[43] Francesco Albergati Capacelli, though himself but a lukewarm fan of the latest trends, could not help wondering:

> What harm would it do if your hair, which you keep neglectfully gathered up in a ribbon, sported for example a simple yet elegant head-dress *à la baigneuse, à la laitière,* or *à la voltaire?* In what way would it prejudice your decorum if you allowed two pretty curls *à la barry* to brush against your neck, or if you wore a fichu that was cut and sewn by one of those many beautiful young girls who create the fichus at Madame Nanette's boutique [Madame Nanette was a French hosier, well known in Milan, whose boutique was opposite the Contrada de' Rastelli]; and if instead of those laces which I see that you use to fasten your shoes, you had a decent pair of those eternal buckles *à l'artois?*[44]

For their part, society's great and good displayed

> a universal weariness with all Italian manufactures, however exact, however ingenious, however clever, and a capricious desire, or rather a frenzied longing, to try out everything that is most curious and most splendid in every form of clothing originating in all the furthest-flung countries, over mountains and seas.[45]

Women, for their part, 'decked out in sumptuous party finery' groaned 'under the weight of gigantic head-dresses, towering crests, crinolines, bracelets and ribbons, and were so loaded down with fine adornments that the royal Prophet might compare them to the most highly honoured and decorated of temples: *filiae eorum compositae, circumornatae, ut similitudo templi* [their daughters were dressed up, with ornaments all around their outfits, looking like temples]'.[46] Such women were bewitched by the 'whole paraphernalia of toilet accessories, the ever changing hairstyles, the varied perfumes, cinnabars and facepaints, the innumerable trimmings given to clothes and quilts as well as a hundred other noble decorative features, the minute arsenal of stucco-work, pendants, broaches, pins, and that portable haberdashery of jewels, bonnets, plumes, veils, lace, sashes and an infinity of other baubles that are in fashion'.[47]

In his guileless astonishment and indignation (backed by considerable first-hand knowledge), the Carmelite friar Pier Luigi Grossi seemed not to remember that 'women only take such great care in dressing the better to make men wish to see them undressed'.[48] If even such 'a most impudent cynic were forced to confess that modesty [*pudore*] was the spice of virtue',[49] the 'lust for novelty' that had infected pious Italy in the final decades of the eighteenth century had caused people to forget that modesty was an 'essential Christian virtue, and its opposite an abominable offence'.[50] A whirlwind of change was overturning the formerly well-ordered and solid virtues of a Catholic people: libertinism, Jacobinism, unbelief, irreligiousness, egalitarianism and contempt for authority. At Parma, perhaps the most Francophile of Italian cities, under the shadow of the Bourbon fleur-de-lis, Bishop Adeodato Turchi (1724–1803) in his All Saints' Day homily in 1794 pointed to 'the wicked love of novelty' as the secret agent of moral corruption, devastating a country already threatened by de-Christianization and teetering on the brink of an 'abyss of perdition'.

> We nowadays bewail a mass of crimes and horrors that seem utterly new and that perhaps no previous century ever witnessed. Yet which century but our own was ever so agitated by a rage for novelty? There is a new way of thinking, a new way of conversing, a new way of acting. It was small novelties that in the beginning opened up this tragic scene. New systems were found pleasing merely because they were new. New words appeared that attenuated people's horror of vice and their appreciation of virtue. Our elders knew not how to live: everything that was old was deemed illicit. Simpletons and libertines were given to believe that in order to be happy old laws, old customs and old maxims had to be replaced by new laws, new customs and new maxims. The spirit of novelty became a rage. Solidity was exchanged for frivolity, honesty for baseness, usefulness for perniciousness.[51]

This perverse and raging love of novelty was abetted by the most irrepressible inconstancy, thereby further augmenting the 'excess of expenditure'[52] with the continual modification of 'fickle fashions' and 'the mutability of sumptuous luxury', making a mockery of the 'tough and Alpine' (Parini) 'fashions of our forefathers', and disparaging the 'deceased centuries'. Fickleness and irrationality, inconclusive *rêverie* and arrogant *raison*. Such disconcerting passion for small futile things, for fake and illusory needs, was unreasonable. The 'universal weariness with all Italian manufactures' was irrational, the uncontrollable 'grand passion' for 'small nothings' and 'light and frivolous objects' was incomprehensible and the capricious and bizarre wish for 'a hundred thousand pretty trinkets' was simply bewildering. Inconclusive childishness and puerile infatuation went hand in hand with 'slothful slackness' and 'excessive delicacy'. The 'refinement' of life's comforts was the goal of 'cultivated' nations, competing 'to raise elegance of taste to the level of a science'. Among the upper classes the 'spirit of delicacy' had led to an Epicureanism that was 'noble and fine', indeed 'honest and decent', in marked contrast to the tumultuous and disorderly pleasures of the uncouth and coarse *nouveaux riches*. Yet it was but a short step 'from delicacy to voluptuousness, from laxness to corruption, from sensitivity to sensuality'. Count Roberti, a former Jesuit and a shrewd observer of the changes taking place during his lifetime, exclaimed:

> One cannot but confess that this sinful flesh, if too much caressed by food, by wine, by sleep, by harmony and by fragrance, can become imperious and prevail over reason. How unjust are certain calculations that offend against liberty and grace![53]

Every gentleman who joined in the headlong rush to frivolous consumption, the search for pleasure in the plentiful supply of material goods, in what is known today as 'unbridled consumerism' but was at that time still called the 'adornments of life', aspired to become 'an ingenious person and thereafter a delicious one'. But this quest had spread far beyond the bounds of the nobility and of the grand bourgeoisie, percolating down to ordinary people and contaminating those of obscure origin and low condition. Mass hedonism was making its first appearance. Even town air was not the same as before.

> What is certain is that, at least in towns, a kind of slothful slackness, breaking a brief bout of work with a long period of idleness, is creeping into storehouses and workshops, not without damaging the arts and not without eliciting complaints from the citizenry. With one voice, the people are asking for bread and for entertainments; they seem to be demanding, as their right, theatre, banquets, public promenades, gambling, dancing and popular assemblies. Each town yearns to boast that it is the home of joyous women and entertaining men. *Terra suaviter viventium* [The land of *bon viveurs*].[54]

Whether in their 'standard of living' or in their manner of dressing, everyone now wanted to 'exceed the boundaries set by birth and station'.

> Life in society nowadays brings unbearable burdens and tyrannical decencies. Indeed, in terms of clothes, it is hard to tell the citizen from the patrician, the rawboned artisan from the wealthy merchant, the disgraceful shrew from the upstanding wife and mother. For the various different conditions, and even the two sexes, conspire to surpass one another in the splendour of their attire, so that finally in the matter of drapery, needlework, fabrics, trimmings and other materials, there is no limit to their ambition, their spite and their rivalry.[55]

The 'science of *savoir vivre*', which in the past only an elite had known and practised and the subtleties of which many 'elders' (ancestors) had known nothing at all, was now within the grasp of all those who, in the universal reshuffling of 'estates' and classes, had managed to get rich.

Holidays were no longer the preserve of an elite nor good food the monopoly of high-born aristocrats. Alongside the two antique and classical cuisines of the people and of the nobility, a third cuisine was emerging and steadily expanding its influence: that of the petty-bourgeois artisans and of the middle classes (that middle class of 'lawyers, merchants and scribes' which Vittorio Alfieri had scornfully dubbed the 'class of the ugliest', 'certainly not a middle class, no, rather upper-plebeian'). This cuisine was in strong contrast to the enlightened, delicate and refined tables of well-bred intellectuals and of aristocrats. On the hills of Bologna

> When summer draws near
> The villas fill up
> With merry brigades
> Who while away the hours
> Atop pleasant hills
> Or at the foot of a valley.
>
> But the affluent and the titled
> Do not venture there alone.
> The traders set up shop –
> Like the vilest of the workmen:
> The tailor and the barber,
> The blacksmith and the junkman.
>
> They go there for the pleasure
> Of merrymaking in company:
> All are eager for a party
> And no one cares to count the cost.
> Each man treats his fellow-guest
> And wallows and devours the fare.
>
> At the table the chase is on
> For the tastiest of morsels.
> Turtles, quail and pigeons,
> And fully flavoured figs,
> With salami, mortadella and foods
> Fried, boiled, stewed or baked.
>
> On occasion a tasty stew
> Of tortellini or of gnocchi
> Is added to the menu: and if
> The hostess so desires,

Foreign wines of every kind,
Even from the isle of Venus.

Course by course the workman's table
Fit for a banquet is arrayed:
And Madame now yields to vanity
And her favours casts abroad.
She begs forgiveness and protests:
'But you have caught me quite off guard!'

There is pie aplenty and for dessert
Candied fruit and sugared almonds
Flowers too, an entire border,
And the most select of fruits.
And as for cheese, there's marzolino
Or parmesan or soft stracchino.

After dinner there is coffee,
With white and black rosolios:
Madame's daughter, with the quiff,
Clasps the glasses or the cups
As her mother fills them brimming
With water of Turkey or of Persia.[56]

THREE

GOOD COOKS AND SKILFUL HAIRDRESSERS

A shrewd observer of the changes in taste and of the various other transformations affecting eighteenth-century civil society commented that 'the era of slack and lazy living that continues today' started when 'effeminacy came into Italy with the harsh clashing of swords, and idleness came with the thundering cannon of foreign armies'.[1] The Jesuit count who made these remarks, Giovan Battista Roberti (1719–86), was an acute observer of new customs and an attentive analyst of changing society. He was also well aware of the fact that French cultural hegemony and French culinary internationalism were closely linked to the military expansionism and to the dynastic politics of the Bourbons, as well as to the lively free-for-all of Parisian intellectual salons. France exported cannon and ideas; in the wake of its bayonets, wherever the *Armée* reached, there soon followed books and cooks, *philosophes* and *chefs de cuisine*. Even treatises on French cooking stressed in their titles the personalized hero worshipping and the unmistakable nationalistic pride of the latest Gallic invasion: *Le cuisinier roial et bourgeois* by Massialot (1691, first Italian translation 1741); *Le cuisinier français* by François Pierre, Sieur de La Varenne (1651, first Italian translation Bologna, 1693). These, the two best-known guides to French cookery, exhibited not only 'the art of good cooking' but also the service of the artist to the king, the culinary national service, the slaughterman-cum-swordsman who speared pheasants and partridges on his spit-blade, the manipulator-inventor (after the Revolution and butter's seizure of power) of happy combinations of new sauces, of new 'mouth munitions'. It is the new *cuisinier* that strides forth, chest out. Indeed, it is the *cuisinier français*, a cook of course, but always French, proudly French, like 'Le Sieur de la Varenne, Escuyer de cuisine de Monsieur le Marquis d'Uxelles'. *Escuyer de cuisine* – no mean cook slaving over a hot stove and bound to the corporatist tradition of the anonymous masters of stoves however aristocratic, but rather a proud esquire for whom the culinary wars waged against deer and wild boar represented a pleasant distraction from the military campaigns of the glorious feudal cavalry of the *conquérants*, of the furious and haughty masters of war of the most powerful and bellicose *armée* in Europe. It is no accident that *Le cuisinier français* sets out a whole long series of 'entrées that can be prepared in the armies or in the country'. *Entrée en guerre / entrée de table*, the start of the fray, the joining of culinary battle at close quarters. And the entrée was indeed the first course after the hors-d'œuvre or soup (now almost vanished from French tables).

'Coal is killing us,' the heroic Carême had exclaimed one day, 'but what matter! A shorter life but a more glorious one!'[2] And for the fatherland and the culinary glory the 'enfants' and the cookery 'brigades', under the guidance of invincible cooks, launched into battle with epic fury: 'patisserie is very difficult to work and very dangerous,' Laguipierre, another famous *maître*, used to say 'and, as a consequence, it is an honourable profession! It is a continual combat!'[3]

Banquets were like battles whose outcome was uncertain: it was essential that the cook, like a seasoned strategist, should be able to fall back on good reserve forces and thereby minimize his risks. He must therefore constantly bear in mind 'this eternal principle, that a gastronomic feast is like an army, you never quite know what you will have on your hands; you have to have splendid reserves!'[4]

Because he had run out of reserves (a consignment of fresh fish had failed to arrive at the right moment) or, according to another version, because of a roast that had turned out wrong, *maître* Vatel had been left no choice but to commit suicide, washing away in his own blood the shame he felt for the festive *débâcle*. For certain virtuoso Gallic cooks, a 'gastronomic feast' could well terminate in a gory act of hara-kiri. The example that had been set by Vatel, 'a man of duty and of etiquette',[5] fortunately remained a noble but isolated case. And the pointlessly squandered talent of Vatel (upon which, however, the impossible to please Marquis De Cussy saw fit to cast doubt) was reborn yet greater than before. The great tradition proceeded onward and upward to attain quite dizzying heights. After the last grim years of the interminable reign of Louis XIV, an era of great table 'décor' and of a style of cuisine that was careful and sumptuous but devoid of 'Epicurean sensualism',[6] after the decline of the Sun King, the leading position of French gastronomy became unchallengeable.

A century later Antoinin Carême, the undisputed master of the age of Napoleon and the Restoration of the Bourbons, stated with touching modesty that France 'is the only country in the world for good food'.[7] Yet the well-founded pride of this leading light did not prevent him from penning several sage remarks about his difficult and strenuous profession, placing emphasis on the close relation between the art of tricking hunger (by confusing the healthy appetite of the stomach with the insidious and perfidious appetite of the palate) and the cunning devices of diplomacy.

Not only were diplomats 'fine appreciators of a good dinner', as Carême put it in one of his 'Aphorismes, pensées et maximes', but 'culinary art provides an escort to European diplomacy'.[8] Not for nothing was it that the 'pastry-making architect' had known employ in the household of Prince Charles-Maurice de Talleyrand, the unrivalled master of the science of survival at any cost and in any circumstance.

It may be a coincidence, but it is reliably ascertained that the great season of French *haute cuisine* began during the negotiations that led to the Treaty of Utrecht and that it received its finishing touches at the tables of the plenipotentiaries. It was the golden age of pastry-cookery too. Carême, whom Lady Morgan considered a 'well-mannered man', a skilful draughtsman and an experimenter of the European culinary schools, harboured no misgivings whatever about this attribution of dates. The great neoclassical reformer of the science of proportions as it applied to flavours had learned architectural principles from a study of the Italian classics – Vignola, Palladio, Scamozzi – and he had made a humble pilgrimage to Vienna, Warsaw, St Petersburg, London, Rome, Naples and even to Switzerland, to learn the secrets of the profession. It may be that he was exaggerating when he wrote that 'there are five fine arts: painting, poetry, music, sculpture and architecture, the main branch of which is pastry-making', but he was well aware of the fact that French pastry-making had attained its sophistication in the kitchens of the plenipotentiaries who had negotiated an end to the War of Spanish Succession.

> In those days it was pastry-cooks who created the greatest delicacies of the court of the most gallant of kings, while playing an active role in society. They were noticed for their elegance. Once diplomacy became an accepted science, that is, after battles were halted, they fanned out all over Europe.[9]

But it was above all during the years of the Regency (1715–23), under the 'sweet authority of the good Regent . . . in the glare of his little suppers',[10] that French cuisine was really launched: 'it is to the cooks whom [Philippe d'Orléans] brought into being and whom he paid and treated so royally and courteously, that the French owed their exquisite eighteenth-century cuisine'.[11] More than a blossoming, it was a bursting forth, an unforeseeable explosion of refinement combined with a lust for life and the subtle pleasure of brilliant conversation. This science of flavours gave the culture of the century an extraordinary verve and imparted enormous impetus to the scintillating ideas of philosophers and intellectual ladies.

> This cuisine, which we now possess in its perfected state, combining skill and simplicity, was a huge, rapid and unhoped-for development. The entire century, or rather all it possessed of wit and delicacy, was seduced. Far from halting or obscuring the intelligence, this cuisine, with its vigour, acted as a stimulus: every serious and fertile matter was now debated and resolved at table. French conversation, which earned for our books of quality their universal

readership, attained its height of perfection at table, during charming soirées.[12]

'The table,' Montesquieu observed, 'contributes not a little to affording us that merriment which, combined with a certain modest informality, is called *politesse*. We avoid the two extremes to which the nations of the South and North are given: we often eat in company, and we do not drink to excess.'[13] This satisfaction with the *politesse* that arose from the table would have appeared misplaced to Giacomo Leopardi, who used to eat on his own (μονοφάγοσ) both by vocation and as a matter of principle. Finding himself, one sultry day in July 1826, in a city renowned for the conviviality of its inhabitants and for its general pleasantness, Leopardi noted in his *Zibaldone*:

> We have abandoned the very natural and joyful custom of the banquet and now speak while we eat. I can hardly believe that at this unique hour of the day when one's mouth is encumbered, when one's exterior speech organs have another occupation (an extremely interesting occupation that it is extremely important to perform well, since it is on good digestion that man's well-being – his good bodily, and hence mental and moral, health – to a great extent depends; and digestion cannot be good unless it is begun in the mouth, as the well-known medical proverb or aphorism says): that precisely this hour of the day, then, should be the one when people speak most; for there are many people who, devoting the rest of the day to study or to solitude for one reason or another, only converse at table, and would be very annoyed if they found themselves alone and silent at that hour. But I, having at heart my good digestion, do not think that it is inhuman of me if, at that hour, I wish to talk the least possible, and if I therefore eat on my own. All the more so since I like to be able to swallow my food in accordance with my own need and not according to that of others, many of whom often devour their food, merely gobbling it up and gulping it down. And if their stomach is happy with such a procedure, it does not follow that mine must also be thus happy, as it would have to be if I ate in company, in order not to make the others wait and to observe the good manners that the ancients, as

I believe, rather neglected in such circumstances: another reason why they were quite right to eat in company, just as I consider that I am absolutely right to eat alone.

Not only did this view enjoy historical documentary support (as Leopardi also pointed out, the ancient Greeks and Romans made a clear-cut distinction between 'eating together' and 'drinking together' and for them 'it was usual to drink together after the meal, as it is nowadays with the English, and such drinking was accompanied at most by a little nibbling at titbits just to sharpen their thirst'), it was also a very respectable opinion, given its impeccable logic and its style of reasoning. It was certainly much more subtle and apposite than certain remarks made by Montesquieu, who, on the subject of eating, did not always manage to avoid banalities and contradictions. 'Dinner,' opined the peerless author of *Lettres persanes*, 'kills one half of Paris; lunch kills the other half.'[14] But he immediately added that 'lunches are innocent; dinners are almost always criminal'.[15]

The cultivated baron from the West exaggerated somewhat, for Paris was 'the capital of the most distinguished sensuality' and at the same time 'of the most disgusting gluttony', just as it was at one and the same time the capital 'of good taste and of bad taste, of high prices and of reasonable prices'.[16] Montesquieu believed, however, that his country was the ideal land in so far as it maintained the best relation with 'good food', because, he wrote, 'it is a fine thing to live in France: food is better than in cold countries and one has a better appetite than in hot countries'.[17] Yet he unconditionally (and quite rightly) approved of those who argued that 'medicine changes with cooking'.[18] Count Roberti, always happy to wax ironic at the expense of the 'mannered Frenchman', was of the opinion that

> the French have a fastidious palate: but Jean-Jacques Rousseau is right to say in *Émile* that 'the French believe they are the only people who know how to eat but I would say that they are the only people who do not know how to eat'; for all that other peoples require in order to eat well is to have good food and a healthy appetite, but the French need a good cook as well. A fine young

Italian gentleman, who lived his life completely à la française, one day complained to me that he was without his French chef, who always accompanied him everywhere on all of his travels: 'I assure you,' he told me, 'I am quite incapable of eating even a boiled chicken unless it has been cooked by him or by a professor similar to him.' What troubles these fine gentlemen do have! For my part, I would be happy to eat not just a chicken, but even a capon, even were it cooked by the steward's wife herself. In the days of Augustus Sicilian cooks were the most highly prized, but today these important men, these highly appreciated domestic chemists, must be French or at the very least Piedmontese. And yet (who would credit it?) the art of cookery in fact arrived in France from Italy during the reign of Henri II, when Italians in great numbers accompanied Queen Catherine de Medici. But the French, who cannot deny this, might well reply with the words of Livy (book XXXIX): *Vix tamen illa quae tunc conspiciebantur, semina erant futurae luxuriae* [Yet those good elements that were only just becoming apparent at the time were the seeds of the forthcoming prosperity]. Nowadays the French reign supreme in the science of flavours, from the North down to the South.[19]

So unless the cook was French, he was not a real cook. For it was only if such 'domestic chemists', such men of the 'science of flavours', were descendants of Vercingetorix that one might speak in terms of culinary art. They must be French, 'or at the very least Piedmontese'. This was why the first cookery book that, after a century of silence, reappeared in Italy (the first edition of the *Arte di ben cucinare* by Bartolomeo Stefani seems to have been the one published in 1662) was *Il cuoco piemontese perfezionato a Parigi* (Turin, 1766), a book that ushered in the interesting and happy Franco-Piedmontese phase in the history of Italian cuisine. It was probably the same anonymous author who wrote *Il confetturiere di buon gusto* (Turin, 1790), which displayed all the delicacies of Piedmontese pastry-making (pastry from Turin, Savoyard pastry Provençal style, Savoy pastry Piedmontese style, biscuits from Savoy, Savoyard biscuits Provençal style . . .). This tradition continued into the nineteenth century with *Il cuoco piemontese* (Milan, 1815); *Il cuoco milanese e la cuciniera piemontese* (Milan, 1859); and the *Trattato di cucina pasticceria moderna credenza e relativa confettureria* (Turin, 1854) by Giovanni Vialardi, assistant chef and pastry-maker to Carlo Alberto and to Vittorio Emanuele II. In the history of Italian cookery this amounted to a rather marginal Piedmontese passage set in the days of the Risorgimento, as peripheral as the little-known kingdom of Sardinia, which only now, after the dazzling exhibition of the Savoys' porcelain and silverware, is at long last beginning to attract a degree of subtler and more sophisticated attention capable of dismantling the old stereotype of highlander kings and coarse valley-dwelling dukes. The architectural sophistication of the eighteenth-century Savoys extended to the exquisite elaborateness of their table and above all to the buffet and to pastry. Such delights were well known to eighteenth-century aristocratic Italy and even to the nobility beyond Piedmont, who looked to the court of Turin as 'a court of arbitration for us', as the Jesuit count G. B. Roberti expressed it, a place 'of much elegance, from where flow not only good cooks but also skilful hairdressers'.[20]

That for a long time no treatises on Italian culinary art were forthcoming throws light on the prolonged and critical transition that accompanied these changes in society. The Italian table (of aristocratic and high-bourgeois circles, obviously) was embarking upon a period of reflection, rethinking and transformation. The old and glorious Renaissance and baroque treatises could not meet the new demands for measured and balanced pleasure. The monumental cookery of the courts and the sumptuous, massive, ostentatious, oppressive and subtly mournful cuisine of the refined, noble and popish tables of the old society did not satisfy the new taste, the need for 'elegant simplicity'.[21] The 'exquisite and solemn luxury' of the eighteenth century, the 'ill-advised prodigality', the 'abundant liberality' of the 'old manner' (all these expressions are employed by G. B. Roberti)[22] now had to come to terms with a new, well-pondered 'taste for elegance'.[23] The eighteenth century continually measured itself against the seventeenth century, and in cookery (as well as in literature) there commenced a time of careful reassessment, a critical process of review and a break with the past. The 'quarrel between the ancients and the moderns' shifted from the writing-desk to the dining-table. The spirit of Arcadia, stepping from the boudoir of 'indolent' women, took up position on the dining-tables of 'extremely soft and delicate' men and of 'very delicious and affected' women.

FOUR

THE PURGED CENTURY

The 'fine arts', casting aside inflated and unwieldy baroque forms, became more nimble, gracious and slender: in the salons the play of perspective opened out on to breezy backcloths, and ceilings revealed azure skies across which glided white, wispy clouds. The interiors of aristocratic houses made a more rational use of space, furniture was slimmed down and its newly lithe and nervous lines glistened with lacquered or inlaid surfaces. Rococo style and in particular sensual and neoclassical poetics demanded noble simplicity, dry decorum. 'Good taste' dictated its new laws to the new 'genius' of the age. In the same way, the reformed cuisine of the Enlightenment gave expression to the *Lebensgefühl* of the fledgling century, its hunger for light, trim and nimble bodies (alert and agile, like the new ideas and spirit) in stark contrast to the previous century's floating, blown-out masses of flesh. There was a new language of gesture and a new sense of body movement to be interpreted. Men's clothes, bulky and redundant, flared from the waist down, were drawn in and streamlined. In the second half of the seventeenth century skin-hugging clothes replaced looser garments, the *culotté* replaced billowing breeches. Men's clothes, which in the seventeenth century had generally been cut in such a way as to make their wearer appear taller, more powerfully built and impressive, shrank to more realistic proportions.

The cuisine of the old society, with its 'patriarchal' dishes, did not satisfy the new taste, the growing demand for 'elegant simplicity'. The 'exquisite and solemn luxury', the 'unruly pomp', the 'ill-advised prodigality', the 'abundant liberality' of the 'old manner' had to come to terms with a new, measured and balanced 'taste for elegance'. The 'taste of the century', the taste of 'this purged century of ours'[1] (as it was dubbed by Francesco Algarotti, Voltaire's 'dear swan of Padua', the most penetrating eye in the eighteenth century, the author of *Congresso di Citera*, a sophisticated connoisseur of art and of everything beautiful), sought to restore balance to the laws of the table through a series of well-pondered and enlightened steps, inventing new utensils, prescribing new rhythms, inaugurating new ceremonies and prohibiting foods deemed not merely obsolete but positively harmful and above all socially improper and vulgar, such as garlic, onion, cabbage and – as was to be expected – cheese. Praise for the 'ordinary sparse table' and its attendant 'healthy simplicity' none the less displeased those who had known the largesse, indeed the grandeur, magnificence, pomp and splendour of the seventeenth-century table. The aged feudal count to whom Abbot Roberti chose to address his letter on 'the luxury of the eighteenth century' argued, without any hesitation, that

> they ate better in the seventeenth century than now, even though the table then offered the eye neither so many sauces, nor so many colours, nor so many shapes, nor so many lying and peculiar names . . . Our calves reared on good-quality milk, our cattle fattened on sweet-smelling hay, our chickens plumping slowly, well fed in the soft slothfulness of their spacious cages, and our large birds and game all contributed to healthy and tasty meals. The dishes that it is your custom to call patriarchal, the choicest of game, surpass all the knowledge of all the cookery schools in current existence. I challenge – as you say – Massialot [author of *Le cuisinier roial et bourgeois*, one of the most important precursors of Regency cuisine], great master of the art of preparing food, to cook for me a young and fleshy woodcock, or a dozen fine plump warblers. The method of regularly eating only the very best meat, fish, vegetables, birds, game and fruit in the season and at the time of day when they are at their fattest or ripest was, and would still be today, an expensive, agreeable and eminently gentlemanly method.[2]

Changes in table-fare were part of a much broader development that was affecting the Italian economy – the emergence of a more realistic financial awareness and of an economic ideal that sought to rationalize exchange and consumption. This exerted a profound influence on the baroque aristocratic style, so attuned to magnificence and to the showy splendour of ceremonial and pomp.[3]

The 'ill-advised prodigality' of the previous century gave way to a 'delicate sumptuousness' that had little inclination for the madness of dissipation and squandering that had light-headedly consumed resources and capital throughout the seventeenth century, scorning any economic logic, out of a mere ostentation of aristocratic grandiosity. People were developing a new relation with food, taking a new look at it. Taste was being transformed, excess and splendour were condemned as evidence of irrational dissoluteness, theories of good taste adopted the yardstick of measured sobriety. Wild ostentation was no longer the best way of demonstrating one's wealth and liberality. Abbot Roberti was of the opinion that

> if to prove wealth it sufficed to spend money, what meal could surpass in luxury the one that was offered by Boullion, minister of state at the French court, during the last century? For Boullion had the grand idea of setting the table with dishes seasoned and studded with gold and silver coins, then inviting and encouraging his dining companions to help themselves copiously with their own spoons and even to use their fingers, fearing not to dirty them.[4]

The new 'taste for elegance' informed a strategy quite different from the 'table tactics', which in any case were changing of their own accord, without the intervention of the 'Caffè' enlighteners, whose 'reform' was confined to ratifying a change that had already occurred, fixing attitudes already widespread, codifying the existing state of things, following the current, in line with social developments.

Saint-Evremond, an old libertine whom an entire generation had regarded as the master of the 'science of pleasures',[5] had, in accordance with his precisely measured hedonism and on behalf of

Epicurus (and under the influence of Horace and Petronius), proposed a programme of moderate and well-adjusted delights, a 'voluptuousness without voluptuousness'.[6] For the wise doctrine of this ancient master, who had died in London in 1703, had insisted that 'sobriety be an economy of the appetite and that the meal that one was having might never harm the one that one would have later'.[7]

It was in this context of a carefully weighed late-baroque review of taste that heavy meats, 'black' flesh (just the kind of meat that was later banished from Italian Enlightenment tables), encountered their first defeat. Oysters and truffles seized power, forcing all the strong dishes typical of ancient aristocratic tables into exile. Poised to redraw the map of 'the geography of greed',[8] Saint-Evremond, Anglo-French aristocrat and insatiable theoretician of perfection, inventor of the 'imaginary woman', after being explored (then translated) with admiring sympathy by Lorenzo Magalotti, the 'Ulysses of Tuscany' (as Francesco Redi called him), penned in verse the order of execution of the old feudal cuisine:

> Let us banish all black meats
> Suffer them no more at our repasts
> Except for two that share the honour
> Of pleasing the palates of the delicate.
> Come hither, ornament of every kitchen
> Birds that none could love too much
> Sand-brown larks and marshy snipe,
> Does one need to speak your names?[9]

Shells, the cold offspring of Thetis, were going to beat the record that birds had set. The palates of the 'delicate' had changed quarter, as fickle as the wind. 'As regards taste', 'oysters' (especially those from Colchester) had succeeded in

> surpassing
> Every flying creature,
> All game, all ragout, all that the famous
> Inventor of Epicure's tomb might boast.[10]

Game birds, game animals, black meats and even the famous stew that its inventor had dedicated to the glorious shades of Epicurus were threatened by the clattering forward march of raw oysters, which in Italy too, as Magalotti recorded in 1682, had taken their place among the 'strange adoptions' of the 'carefree modern carvery'.[11]

Along with the tomb of Epicurus, 'every flying creature' and 'all game' had now entered a funereal twilight zone. Potent symbols of feudal conviviality and of barbaric aggression, these glorious black and bloody meats suffered the affront of having to bow to the soft, bloodless and gelatinous pulp-like flesh of oysters and to the ambiguous smell of dark and dank earth exuded by the melancholy and depressingly venereal truffles, subterranean fruits that fed on darkness, night-time dews, opaque saps.

> Oysters, you have won the day,
> Truffles alone shall be more prized.[12]

It is striking that the decline of sumptuous Renaissance and baroque cuisine marked an end to the great hunts and the downfall of everything that darted through the air or dashed across the ground, everything that moved, flexed, leaped, expended energy or lived in close animal familiarity with the rain, the wind and the sun. Striking indeed that the century of intellectual light, the enemy of darkness and shadows, should prefer to seek nourishment from gelid, inert, corpse-like organisms, ripped from water or from sterile bulbs that hated light, fed on the dank lunar darkness of great autumnal forest subsoil. Striking indeed, though not paradoxical, that Robespierre, the virtuous, rigorous, abstemious and vegetarian Robespierre (who shared with the ascetics the 'sad singularity of eating nothing but vegetables'),[13] had the royal game of Versailles butchered, decapitating both the undulating silhouette of the Queen, and the heavy King, that lover of the arts of Vulcan, specialist in the technology of fire.

These new men, these French-trained followers of the Enlightenment, relentless in their condemnation of the excesses and trifling of the baroque century, these implacable demolishers of the old 'manner', happy in their small, elegant but soberly furnished rooms, in *cabinets* and in snug well-lit studies, would have deemed it the depths of bad taste when on a visit to Madrid to descend into the *buen ritiro* of a Spanish–Italian noble of the previous century, into the sweet-scented cavern of Luigi Guglielmo Moncada d'Aragona of the dukes of Montalto, a splendid Sicilian baron who in Spain had become a 'grande' and who in 1664, after the death of his second wife, had attained the rank of cardinal. His astonishing *Boveda*, shrouded in a perpetual mist of perfumes, the supreme example of unbridled sensuality and of turbid Arabic and Mediterranean laxness, would have struck terror into any enlightener chancing to stumble upon it. The man who appeared to Lorenzo Magalotti to be the high priest of aromas, a magician of olfactory delirium, the 'great protecting genius of smells',[14] would have struck the men of the 'Caffè' as a sort of Levantine caliph.

> It was a kind of subterranean passage that he had had excavated under his house in Madrid, with the express intention of providing for himself and his friends a place in which to spend the scorching hours of summer... The walls were white, without any decorations other than mirrors. There were large marble tables, bearing vases of fresh flowers, always the most sweet-smelling of the season. Beneath the tables, tubs rather than basins full of scented rushes, arranged in various guises and all of excellent quality. Against the main façade, a huge cupboard stood against the wall of the vault, with various shelves. One shelf was completely covered with *buccheri* [a kind of scented earthen vase] from the Indies, another with those from Maya, another with ones from Estremoz. Another shelf was given over to porcelains. All the vessels were uncovered, and all full of vinegars and flower waters prepared in the manner best known to the Cardinal. At the windows hung curtains made of Dutch fabric, and on the bed a blanket of amber skins hemstitched with a lining of light silk. Between two and three o'clock in the morning, when the Cardinal was on the point of waking, Francisco, one of his valets who had been trained from childhood in perfumery, would go down into the Boveda, bearing two or three large silver syringes, one full of vinegar and the others of enriched waters, and would then go to work. Like Dutch boatmen when they spray the sails of their small craft so that they will hold the

wind better, Francisco pressed from his syringes a continual mist until everything was impregnated, not only the air but also the flowers in their vases, the *buccheri* (though only those from Portugal) and the curtains hanging at the windows. The vinegar, however, he sprayed only on the brick floor. Having completed this job of sprinkling, he would then throw open the large tabernacle that, as the Marquis of Grana related to me, was a veritable glory: and it was then that the Cardinal would descend.[15]

The gap was widening between Spain with its Mozarabic ceremonials and eighteenth-century Italy, now in hot pursuit of northern patterns of development. Spanish fashion was on the wane, its language was in decline, its perfumes, aromatic jellies, cream pastes, candied fruits, honeyed and drugged drinks like *aloxa* were all forgotten. *Candiero* too was vanishing, though Lorenzo Magalotti, a man straddling South and North, an explorer of the cultures of 'non-barbarian Europe', one day wrote the recipe out in verse:

> Take some egg yolks barely cooked
> Beat them in polished porcelain,
> And if you wish for something sovereign
> Beat and toss them to your utmost;
> Then sprinkle in a deal of sugar
> Certainly more than just a pinch;
> Now you take a huge *bucchero*:
> You cannot do such things by halves!
> A bit of musk and lots of amber,
> Twenty, thirty wisps of jasmine,
> Peel a pair of little lemons
> Just to please the ticklish palate.[16]

Having discovered England, the great voyager in the service of Cosimo III turned his back for a while on Iberian creams and seemed to forget his powders and pastilles, his 'flower chocolates' and his glacé compotes. Seduced by the 'beautiful enchanted island', he heaped praise on the recipe of *'content*, an English dish', just then reaching the continent.

Thus from England is arrived
At just the right moment
A pleasant new concoction:
A whitish paste,
Sweet-smelling,
And runny,
A comforter of three senses.
A delicate
And perfumed paste
Reaching the blood in just an instant.
Suffice it to say
That its happy creator
Named it *Content*.
Now listen. Weigh
A pound in equal measure
Of rice and almond flour.
So far so simple:
Harder work
And stranger is what's next . . .
Take purest rainwater
Just as nature
Has it plummet from the sky.
But it must be boiling
It must be scalding
There must be plenty to dilute.
So dilute this thick milk paste
Combining flour
Of rice and almonds.
'Tis proof against
The sloth of delicate palates
That long for roses free of thorns.[17]

Mixed with 'manna from Caracas' (that is to say, Chocolate), sprinkled with amber and then poured into a porcelain vase, decorated with flowers, this 'proud jelly' from the shores of Albion was ready to eat.

A Catholic libertine who had breathed the air of the most prestigious courts of Europe, whose 'lordly style . . . owed something to his high birth' and to 'his familiarity with the world' (A.

M. Salvini), a cultural middleman, an importer of Iberian and French novelties yet proud of the great Roman and Tuscan tradition and where necessary critical of the more questionable aspects of foreign cultures, Magalotti, this *Florentin*, with his slight Roman accent, his infallible eye and prodigious nose that from a range of excellence always selected the very best, was also a master of fashion and an exquisite counsellor to gentlemen and to noble ladies on the matter of gloves, fabrics, wigs, porcelain and perfumes. But he was also an eminent art *connaisseur*, a 'natural philosopher' ever curious to learn of nature's freaks and foibles, a polyglot and translator of the rarest oriental languages, a gentleman 'supported' by Grand Duke Cosimo III and a member of his Council of State, a Galilean revisionist, at home in Oxford and at the Royal Society. Indeed, Magalotti was one of the first Italians (foreshadowing the Anglomania of the eighteenth century) to fall in love with Merry England, the 'beautiful enchanted island, / Beloved seat / Of fine weather and enjoyment'.[18]

Although he was perfectly capable of dining at home, seated at a 'small table' by the fire, on 'two spoonfuls of soup, four mouthfuls of mince, a cooked apple and that's all',[19] Magalotti appreciated 'fine Parisian tables' and the 'genius of the [French] nation' as revealed in their 'delicacies for eating'. During his stay in Paris in 1668 he was struck by the 'cleanliness of the kitchen and of the stores' of the *traitteur* (innkeeper) De Noier, as well as by the 'exquisiteness' of his luxury inn, situated at the gates of the capital, in the 'village of Saint-Cloud'.

> This house is one of the greatest attractions for the young people of Paris, because all year round they can come at whatever hour they like and in any number they wish and in less than half an hour they are served for the number of gold coins that they wish to spend per head. The dining-rooms are hung with tapestries, paved with marble, furnished with resting couches, comfortable seats and other noble furniture, while the cornices of the vaults are full of earthen pots from Turkey, *buccheri* and porcelains so crowded together that the vases touch one another, and with glistening crystals, linen from Flanders and silver cutlery. Every dish served is embellished with flowers in season, with ice and white jam, candied fruits, white

jellies, dishes enhanced with amber: in short, with every refinement, cleanliness and gallantry. [20]

Returning from Spain, it was the smells that remained indelibly etched on his heart. He arrived back in Italy 'with the frenzy of smells in his head, and with a library of recipe books, given to him by the Infanta Isabella, by Cardinal de Moncada, and by so many other Spanish and Portuguese lords and ladies'.[21] Bewitched by the jasmine of Catalonia and by the powders of Andalusia and Castile, by jasmine-flavoured and citrus-flavoured chocolate, by the sharp and crackling taste of glacé chocolate and by the much softer one of chocolate flavoured with frangipane, however much he wandered the roads of both civilized and barbarous Europe (even visiting Lapland and Sweden), he would continue to move in a permanent haze of sweet Iberian scents. On his third journey to Flanders, having struck up an acquaintance with the mythic Duke of Montalto (alias Cardinal Moncada), he managed to bribe his valet and thus succeeded in copying the secret recipes of the voluptuous Spanish 'grande' who would have clysters prepared from sweet-smelling saltless waters and keep them inside himself all day long.

FIVE

HEAVY AND VISCOUS MEATS

A new taste, a new poetics and a new style were introducing order, measure and moderation into areas where the excesses and extravagances of the baroque imagination had created bulky, majestic and bombastic cascades of main dishes, marvels of decoration, cream-syringed rhetoric, multiple roasts *à surprise*, batter-gilded meats, monstrous amber-scented pies, sumptuous glacé emblems, ornamented apotheoses and gelatinous tapestries of liquefied lard. The poetics of hyperbole and heaping high (indeed, of *acumulación caotica*) were replaced by refined sobriety and by rationally balanced and didactically pragmatic 'good taste'. Cookery was embarking upon a classicizing phase of even-handed restoration, chipping away gently at the thick incrustations of the past, the 'stale Gothicisms'[1] and the corrupt taste of the seventeenth century, turning aside from the messy heaps that the excesses of baroque fantasy had cast up. The 'taste Reformation'[2] extended to the new programme for the dietary improvement of the human machine: 'Reform cookery!'[3] became the rallying cry of Pietro Verri and his group. Proceeding by well-calculated and enlightened steps, the 'taste of the centruy'[4] refashioned table discipline and ushered in new procedures and previously unknown ceremonials. With kid-glove despotism, new styles were proposed that bristled with 'luminous truths' fit for 'men of enlightenment', the new wave of nimble philosophers so unlike those of the Aristotelian tradition, used to 'arguing about the *universale a parte rei*, about quiddity and other grave trifles and ravings of human feeble-mindedness'.⁵ Banished wholesale from the new science were the 'barbarian words' of the old Aristotelian and scholastic discourse, the abstruse categories of formal logic, the oppressive 'yoke of that science of terms'⁶ (*barbaras* and *baraliptons* being the formal equivalent of indigestible and corrupt baroque heaps). And when they sat down to table, the new intellectuals preferred to draw on modern categories of food that might help them to liberate themselves from the 'coarse nourishment' and the hazy drugs of the past and from the 'soporific and sedative' narcotic cuisine of bygone feudal generations. The triumph of coffee, rich in 'reviving properties', appeared to underscore the reawakening and the liveliness of eighteenth-century intellectuals by 'brightening the soul, rousing the mind . . . infusing the blood with a sal volatile that quickens its movement, thins it, lightens it and in a certain manner revives it', 'being of particular use to persons who make few movements and who cultivate the sciences'.⁷

The 'moderns' summoned the bloated baroque and Asiatic intemperance to appear before the tribunal of good taste, before the enlightened table of reformed *nouvelle cuisine*. In the villa of the modern gentleman the new *ratio ciborum* (order in the serving of food) took the form of a measured succession of refined, sober yet exquisite pleasures.

> The table is as delicate as it can possibly be; the food is all healthy and easy to digest; there is no ostentatious over-abundance but everything necessary to give satisfaction. Heavy or viscous meats, garlic, onions, strong drugs, salted dishes, truffles and other such substances poisonous to human nature are totally proscribed from this table. Their place has been mainly taken by the meat of fowl and of chickens, by green vegetables, by oranges and their juice. The flavours of these foods are exquisite but not strong: every food that acts powerfully on the palate to some extent deadens the said palate and deprives it of an infinite number of more delicate pleasures. Furthermore, every food that powerfully stimulates the palate acts equally strongly on the tunics of the ventricle and of the intestines, and this can occasion an infinity of ills that can repay with huge interest the pleasure of the sensation experienced. Wines

harvested on the neighbouring hills are very tasty and not too strong so that, when mixed with a little bit of water, with their slight acidity, they resemble lemonades and are a delicious drink assisting speedy digestion. No strong-smelling food is allowed at our table and all vegetables that release an evil smell when they rot are proscribed. This is also why cheeses and cabbages of every species are banned. Such is our meal, which we round off with an excellent cup of coffee, satisfied, sated and not oppressed by the kind of coarse nourishment that only puts the mind to sleep and spreads boredom throughout our company, which, indeed, quite to the contrary, after our meals seems to revive with general mirth.[8]

There could hardly be a more revealing snapshot of the reformed eating habits of the nobility than this description, dating from 1764, of new villa pleasures. It gives a valuable and precise outline of the overhauled table manners adopted by a lively and elegant society caught in the process of reshaping and reinventing itself as it marks itself out from the past. The distance covered from baroque eating habits appears considerable, given the insistence on delicacy, lightness, measure ('everything necessary to give satisfaction') and the rejection of clashing tones, of violent flavours, of thick and acrid smells. It all seems a far cry from the 'ostentatious over-abundance', the 'ostentation and vain magnificence' of the seventeenth-century meal. For the 'man of good taste who sought after truth' and who could on no account give in to bizarre and unseemly dreams or to grotesque illusions, nor blunt his intellectual verve and alacrity with 'coarse nourishment', an 'easy' digestion was essential. A 'ready digestion' also needed encouragement from wines that had not only to be 'not too strong' but were watered down to resemble fizzy lemonades. People turned their noses up at local products. 'I do not like our best wines and would prefer a mediocre wine from Austria than the best wine from Lombardy,' Pietro Verri wrote to his brother Alessandro on 26 October 1771. 'Our wine is imbibed in order to become drunk; the other kind is a spirituous lemonade, that makes one merry but nothing more.'[9]

Drugs suspected of 'overheating' were prohibited, as were over-salted and over-peppered foods and truffles ('poisonous to human nature'). Flavours should be 'exquisite but not strong', juxtaposed rather than amalgamated, coupled rather than mixed, and certainly on no account blended.

All 'heavy and viscous' meats were proscribed and meat consumption, as F. Braudel pointed out, declined sharply in the eighteenth century. Modern taste shifted in favour of poultry and fowl: farmyard animals and small game were preferred to pungent-flavoured large game.

According to Vincenzo Tanara, even peacock, dislodged by the tenderer turkey (the 'India cock'), had been relegated by the second half of the seventeenth century to a decorative role at wedding meals and it gradually vanished altogether from eighteenth-century menus. However, the *pavo cristatus* (crested peacock), 'given the splendour of its colours, the most magnificent of all gallinaceous birds', was probably still available under the counter: it certainly left Pellegrino Artusi with the 'memory of meat that, in the case of youngish birds, was quite excellent'. Right into the second half of the seventeenth century fantails were still considered delicacies. Lorenzo Magalotti, a man of transcendental taste, liked fantails so much that he felt obliged to send one to his friend Francesco Redi, along with one of his own recipes:

> A young plump peacock caught in the wild,
> dancing rings round thrushes and buntings:
> this is what I send you, my dearest Redi,
> king of Courtesy, for the soberest of feasts.
>
> Your taste being so expert and so refined
> you will know how best to cook the bird
> for as a master you would scarce be fool enough
> to eat it boiled or drowned in a sauce.
>
> The recipe: take a thick chunk of fresh lard
> whose rind is dyed Brazil-wood red

and was reared on the slopes of the Alps
making the lard thick and plentiful.

With a knife cut the lard into strips
quite as fine as vermicelli:
for the finer you slice it
the tastier your lard strips will be.

Having carefully plucked the bird clean,
now sit down and, trapping it beneath you, begin,
with needle poised, to stuff this multicoloured
marvel both trousers and doublet.[10]

This was a far cry from the large quarries that the nobility had been accustomed to bring back from their baroque hunts, the red and bloody, pungent-tasting meats of large quadrupeds, wild boar, deer. Gone were the days when fallow deer were slaughtered daily at the court of the Medicis, during the hunts at Artimino. Over forty were sometimes slain each day, with the participation of the 'young princesses' and the ladies, and then shared out after the massacre between the 'courtier lords' who ate the noble parts while the innards and heads ended up on the tables of the gamekeepers and scullery boys – 'giblets' for 'kitchen barons'.[11]

In the lax and delicate seventeenth century Francesco Redi's sophisticated table companions would have been horrified if they had known that that 'thin, dry, lanky and emaciated'[12] Grand Duke and chief physician indulged in adventurous gastronomic experiments using fallow-deer brains. For there circulated at court a 'certain ancient, obstinate and worse than heretical belief, upheld by these scoundrels [kitchen staff and hunt assistants], according to which the brain of the fallow deer was a very bad thing indeed, repulsive to eat and very harmful to human health. As a result, whether out of civility or out of fear, there was not in court a single gentleman who would venture to have fallow-deer brain served at his table.'[13]

Yet the inexhaustible anatomist from Arezzo, an unflinching dissector of snakes, worms and toads, 'perpetual persecutor of the most disgusting, the most sordid parts of nature' (Magalotti), one day found himself unable to resist the temptation to remove a fallow-deer brain from his dissection table and to cast it sizzling into a frying-pan. Redi wrote the following lines to Dr Iacopo del Lago in September 1689 (at the height of the hunting season) from the Grand Duke's estate at Artimino:

> Born into this world to discover beautiful and useful things, I have in the last few days held in my hands some of these fallow-deer brains and have been able to observe how they are made. Appearing to me to be beautiful, well fashioned, plump and substantial, I took the risk, even though my servant was ashamed of bringing such Lutheran villainy into the kitchen, of having a first-rate panful fried in virgin lard. They were brought to my table piping hot and well roasted and it was with exceeding relish that I gobbled up almost all of them. After repeating this safe and careful experiment many times over, I judged that the brain of the fallow deer is a noble thing indeed, extremely tasty and healthful and much better than the brain of pigs or calves, not to say better than dolphins' brains, which, in my view, are the very best of all possible brains, considering that one can eat them during Lent and other compulsory fasts.[14]

Count Verri, however much he worshipped Galileo, would certainly never have felt inclined to attempt the 'safe and careful experiment' made by the indefatigable Francesco Redi. Redi, after all, was an experimenter in the Galilean tradition and could take the credit for demolishing the thousand-year-old myth of spontaneous generation and for exploding other archaic beliefs much more stubborn even than that regarding the harmfulness of fallow-deer brain.

Once the initial misgivings had subsided, the court of the Medicis greedily fell upon the cerebral lobes of these noble quadrupeds.

> As it was my custom to preach for the public good, I lauded the merits of my new discovery. It thus became so well known even in the most secret of chambers and antechambers as an invention that had been made

By a man such as myself of a talented mind

that people immediately began greedily to demand fallow-deer brains as a strange and new delicacy; and before long they were being served at all the finest tables.[15]

Then something odd happened. The entire court of Cosimo III fell under the spell of these anatomical and gastronomic experiments. Hacking and grubbing around among the innards, guts and other base parts of these noble fallow deer, another overwhelming discovery came to light. After countless efforts, a blue-blooded high-ranking marquis finally managed to locate such a mysterious and unthinkable delicacy that the previous discovery made by the distinguished chief physician, albeit sensational, paled by comparison. As Francesco Redi, clearly a sarcastic old wag as well as the master of the new science, pretended to lament:

> In this world there is no joy that is not accompanied by some pain or at least by some displeasure. Great might indeed have been my glory, were it not for the fact that, at the very same time, another very tasty discovery had been made in a southerly and hitherto uncharted region of the fallow deer. Indeed, the distinguished Marquis Clemente Vitelli, the first gentleman of the Chamber of the Grand Duke, had, through his unassisted brilliance, discovered that fallow-deer offal are far nobler, tenderer and tastier than the offal of any other brute beast in vogue in the kitchens of contemporary gluttons. Only yesterday morning, to attenuate my brainless pride, he presented me with a dish from his very own table, which, to confess with due devotion the whole truth, was exceeding excellent.[16]

Two generations later such reckless gastronomic trifling with the intestines and innards of fallow deer, with their southernmost or northernmost portions, would have been dismissed as the monstrous whims of extravagant minds not yet illuminated by the light of rediscovered 'good taste'. But Redi's time was still one of controversial discoveries, a time marked by that *fin de siècle* crisis that left its impress even on the uncertain and confused amalgam of edible delicacies and on the criss-crossed web that stretched between the old forms of gluttony and its latest refinements, between medieval meaty morsels and exotic novelties. China and the New World were poised to make a spectacular entrance into the Eurocentric tradition of Tuscan and Italian taste.

SIX

THE STRANGE NEW ADOPTIONS OF LISTLESS GLUTTONY

Dutch, English, Spanish and French vessels, returning from the extreme West or from the distant East, unloaded on to the docks of old Europe bales and crates of new and exciting products: Indian herbs, subtropical powders, disconcerting flowers, unthinkable meats, unpredictable fruits, unknown or barely known tubers, peculiar vegetables, tobacco and cocoa, vanilla and quinquina, peppers and swallows' nests, coffee and tea, tulips and jasmines from Goa, armadillos and turkeys, areca nut and catechu.

In the spice-shops of Leghorn, which struck Usbeck-Montesquieu as 'the most flourishing city in Italy' and 'proof of the genius of the dukes of Tuscany',[1] there arrived in 1679 a drug of an unusually composite flavour. Like a super-concentrate of several other tropical spices, 'with a rind similar to coarse cinnamon, it was dispatched from Cadiz to Signore Cestoni under the name of "all spices", and it seemed to possess, in its range of flavours, the same privilege as that drug or aromatic seed brought back from the West Indies and called by the Spanish *Pimienta de Chapas*'.[2] It was Lorenzo Magalotti who introduced this unknown berry, rather imprecisely baptized 'new spice', to Francesco Redi. It struck the superintendent of the Grand Duchy's 'foundry' as a 'gallant drug' and he identified a whole spectrum of different tastes: 'that of carnations, first of all, that of nutmeg, secondarily, that of cinnamon, in third place, that of citron, the smell of musk, the scent of amber and the gentle suavity of sugar'.[3] When chewed, these seeds released other aromatic flavours reminiscent of juniper berries and – though somewhat milder – of black peppercorns. This original 'Chiapa pepper', which in New Spain was usually included among the ingredients for chocolate, did not meet with the same success in Europe that certain other herbs from the Far East enjoyed. If the impact on Europe of 'Chinese fennel', 'not very unlike our sweet fennel, yet not so sharp and with some hints of aniseed',[4] proved rather short-lived, tea enjoyed an enormous success. Two other 'strange and extremely precious herbs' from the 'great empire of China' remained suspended in the magic limbo of talismans, hovering between legend and reality:

> one of them, called *pusu*, makes the life of men immortal; the other, known as *ginseng*, although it does not contain nearly enough vigour to impart immortality, is none the less so valorous that throughout the entire span of life it can help us to remain healthy, joyous and free of illnesses. There is no doubt that these two herbs must have been contained in great quantity in the great cauldron

> *In which Médée placed her father-in-law to fry*
> *To retrieve him from the claws of old age.*[5]

'Mystic gluttons'[6] could saunter around the shops of Armenian and Jewish traders, among stores and warehouses, hunting out the 'strange new adoptions of listless modern gluttony' capable of 'representing to their minds several degrees of spiritual delicacy'. An 'alphabet' of edible 'hieroglyphs' enriched with yet new marvels the already bursting cupboards and spice-crammed pantries of the old continent. Busy as always, the Jesuits traded and did business, imported and sorted tobacco, quinquina ('Jesuits' powder', as it was then called, or 'Cardinal De Lugo's powder') and cocoa. Armed with unheard-of temptations, rare and enticing goods or with such marvellous powders as quinine, they seduced the spirits of both the powerful and the plebs. Politics ogled at ship holds and at larders, chocolate became an instrument of religious ingratiation, of edifying penetration, a new delicacy offered up *ad maiorem Dei gloriam*. The culinary scene became tangled, displaying a strange brew of archaic leftovers and modern exoticism: 'thrush claws toasted in candle flame; heads of woodcocks, split open and grilled; raw oysters; sprouting fallow-deer antlers, bear paws, swallows' nests from Cochin-China; tea; coffee; ketchup; catechu; . . . the suavest of liquefactions . . . sorbets and glacé chocolates'.[7]

An 'ingenious invention of modern gluttony, always greedy for novelties' – such was Francesco Redi's considered judgement on the fast-spreading vogue for the nests of certain birds from the Far East, served up as food. This was one of a series of recent sophisticated culinary discoveries that, as the Grand Duke and chief physician put it, 'were the more prized the further away they came from'.[8]

> There are certain little birds, rather similar to swallows, that build their little whitish nests in the reefs of the sea of Cochin-China, using a material not unlike fish glue. These nests are torn from the rocks to be sold at a considerable price to embellish banquets that would be considered base and unimpressive were they not enhanced by this bizarre dish, which, when it is skilfully prepared by a knowledgeable chef, is indeed really appetizing. And one of the ways of cooking it is to soak the nests in a good capon or veal stock until they soften and swell up to their proper size. Then they are cooked in this stock and served with butter, cheese and various kinds of spice.[9]

In France certain fastidious palates had become so sophisticated that, even when 'eating in the dark', they could unfailingly tell the difference between 'a breast of pheasant and a breast of capon, a breast of common partridge and a breast of grey partridge'. In France, 'one of the nations that knows a little more about eating than people generally do in Italy', Lorenzo Magalotti had encountered skilled *connaisseurs* and 'gluttons so infallible that they could tell if the chef had cooked the grey partridge on one stove rather than on another. They could even tell if the chef, once the partridge had begun to cook and when their gravy was already beginning to ooze over their skin, had removed them from the stove thereby causing their gravy to cool a little and to assume a *je ne sais quoi* of rottenness that, once they had been put back to fry again, had rendered them,' as he put it, '*détestables du dernier détestable.*'¹⁰

The 'new adoptions' of late-eighteenth-century cuisine, poised between the baroque and the rococo, were a 'studied gift of listless, luxuriant if not luxurious Europeans'¹¹ who yearned for far-flung novelties, for exotic titbits to pamper their eyes, noses or palates. Such novelties and frenzied passions peaked suddenly and then equally suddenly melted away. This was what happened with 'terra japonica' or 'terra catechu', also known as 'cutch', which 'the Portuguese called "cacciunde" and the French "cachou", but which, among us Italians, remained or, for all I know, became "casciù" or "cacciù"'.¹² Many people in Florence believed it to be a 'kind of botched muck made from oriental chocolate'.¹³ Magalotti was the first to extract 'water of catechu', which, 'whether in its pure state as neat water or used in sorbets, surpassed all other summer drinks'.¹⁴ It was a kind of delicately perfumed earth, giving off 'a fragrant scent, which arose so surreptitiously that it vanished into the parched air and your nose could not track it down, even if you tried. But as soon as you placed a little in your mouth, abetted by the moistness of the tongue, the taste became plainer from inside.'¹⁵

Ephemeral spirals of perfumes so ethereal that they melted into nothing: these and many other treasures were the outcome of a voluptuous imagination rather than a product of the senses. Indeed, in the case of this oriental extract as in that of many other new-found delicacies,

> the first time that one tastes such things, or that one hears speak of them, since no one has been warned that they are held to be such remarkable delicacies, nobody likes them. The more sophisticated soul, however, is more inquisitive and better informed, and does not stop at the mere taste of the thing itself, but falls in love with it on the strength of hearsay. Such souls are well disposed and, long before the real taste of the thing touches them, invest it with this imaginary tastiness so that when at last they approach it, they taste the thing as they imagined it would be and not as in fact it is; so, taking pleasure in its image, believe they take pleasure in the thing

itself. As regards Bibbiena, who was later made cardinal, a modern writer and expert in secret information has written: 'He sometimes felt the inclination, during the course of a meal, to make such sauces that no previous chef would ever have imagined. He would set about his work and always managed to please his guests, either because he really was a master of the art of pandering to taste, or because those who had to judge his work helped by deceiving themselves.'[16]

The 'delicate' spirits of this flagging rococo and baroque age, those who fell in love 'on trust' and the visionaries who, working in their internal laboratories, distilled imaginary sweetmeats, were the last representatives of a species that (despite appearances) had become extinct by the middle of the eighteenth century. As typical products of a turn-of-the-century crisis, they failed to be reincarnated in the *philosophes*, nor were they resurrected in the (lighter and headier) flavours of eighteenth-century culinary rationality. There was even less hope of rebirth for the voracious ghost of Polyphagus, that 'great glutton', that belly on legs who had waddled his way through the palaces of the nobles and the French court in the age of Louis XIII and Richelieu, disguised as 'Seigneur Panphagus'. Francesco Fulvio Frugoni lifted 'the great Epicure of this court' from La Mothe le Vayer's *Banquet sceptique*, and placed him in his own Bacchanalian melodrama, *L'Epulone*. In *Cinq dialogues faits à l'imitation des Anciens, Par Oratio Tuberus*, Eraste says:

> I had observed him throughout the entire meal proceeding so rapidly and with such vigour that in truth I believed that, just like deer, goats and sheep, he had several bellies rather than one, and that like hedgehogs, cockroaches and locusts, he possessed in these bellies supplementary teeth, in order to chew his food a second time: for otherwise I cannot comprehend how, possessing only a single belly, any man would not have burst, had he not been able to open and close himself by means of buttons, like the inhabitants of the moon.[17]

In the years when Panphagus haunted the tables of the *hôtels particuliers* (great private mansions) of France, eminent cardinals and other Italian ecclesiastical authorities, when fasting was obligatory, resorted to ingenious culinary deceptions, which, by tricking the eyes, concealed forbidden foods under innocent guises. Counter-Reformation greed was particularly ingenious, managing to smuggle on to the dining-table flavoursome but forbidden and censured meats by cleverly manipulating shapes and colours. Francesco Ridolfi, president of the Accademia della Crusca, wrote to Francesco Redi, regarding the apparent light-heartedness of his famous dithyramb 'Bacco in Toscana':

> One must be careful not to be taken in by appearances. I remember seeing on fast days, at banquets for great ecclesiastics, where scandal was to be avoided, white soups, red mullet, sole, trout: but the soups turned out to be finely minced capon, the mullet grey partridge, the sole black partridge and the trout pheasant, though all the food was arranged to look like fish.[18]

Besides, one could certainly not force all church people, great and small, to subject themselves, like the erudite Jesuit Tommaso Sanchez, to icy and bracing exercises in abstinence, just to avoid voluptuous and sweet temptation. Sanchez, a fine legal mind on all matters regarding marriage and an eminent expert on the most minor of illicit sexual acts, had studied 'these questions for thirty years of his life, sitting on a marble seat, never eating either pepper, or salt, or vinegar, and when he was at table to dine, always keeping his feet in the air'[19] ('salem, piper, acorem respuebat. Mensae vero accumbebat alternis semper pedibus sublatis'). We do not know, in fact, what exactly it was that Sanchez did eat. Given his perfect integrity, it has to be assumed that he avoided meats with too warming an effect and that he took care to steer clear of stag antlers which, variously prepared, always featured in the meals of the unconsecrated. Antlers were to be feared like a fragment from the abyss, *maxime vitandus* (to be avoided whenever possible) like a satanic mouthful. 'Tender antlers,' if Francesco Redi is to be believed, 'are delicacies at the banquets of the great, and chefs use them to prepare a variety of very appetizing little dishes. They use hard antlers to prepare several sorts of jelly very tasty to the palate.'[20] This 'custom of greed',[21] with its many offshoots in seventeenth-century pharmacopoeia, betrayed a veiled belief in the aphrodisiac properties of the antler and of the penis of the stag, a beast of quivering lasciviousness. Redi, in his 'Preghiera e sacrificio a Venere', in hot pursuit of 'lascivious shadows' and 'summertime follies', abandoned himself to voluptuous dreams and thereby caught a glimpse of a *pervigilium Veneris* (vigil in honour of Venus) in which, atop the 'holy fire', there burnt 'laudanum, incense, cinnamon and saffron', while to the goddess Ciprian were offered

> the prized root
> of the illustrious satyrion and,
> of the fecund hart of Etruria, the filthy genital.[22]

As a culinary tradition, the antler of this much envied beast withstood the collapse of kingdoms, social earthquakes, far-reaching changes in taste and dietary revolutions, at least until the Restoration of the Bourbons. Stag antlers reappeared as a 'food seasoning' on a par with butter, parmesan and dry mushrooms (under the 'general condiments' heading) in *Gianina ossia La Cuciniera delle Alpi* (Rome, 1817, vol. i, p. 45), a virtuoso culinary rhapsody finely balanced between the *ancien régime*, Romanticism and the Congress of Vienna, and written by the industrious and imaginative Francesco Leonardi.

On the other hand, one would search in vain among the 'productions of the four seasons' or in contemporary menus for viper's jelly or pulp, meat that since the earliest of times had been attributed with the property of considerably lengthening the span of human life. According to Pliny, the Macrobians, renowned for their longevity, were formidable consumers of viper meat. In the western world, the home of scientific medicine and the exact sciences, the rich and powerful ordained that this life-prolonging (and, as regards women, beauty-giving) meat should be fed to all farmyard animals destined for their table. Neither princes nor kings felt any inclination to end their days prematurely or to run too rapidly through the brief store of years that (in common with other mortals) they had at their disposal. They therefore gave orders that all fowl bred for their banquets should be fed on viper meat. As the 'libertine' La Mothe le Vayer – the man who, according to René Pintard, had devised the 'most audaciously sceptical sayings of the seventeenth century' – had written: 'the princes of Europe feed on vipers the fowl that they themselves then consume'.[23] This 'feeding on viper meat',[24] at one remove, transferred into the meat of domestic fowl, rendered the meals of the princes not only more tasty but also more magical and hence more appetizing. To eat these meaty talismans with reverence and passion not only enhanced the pleasure of the meal before one but also increased the number of years devoted to the pleasures of this world.

The therapeutic myth regarding viper meat (like the culinary myth regarding stag antlers) survived into the early decades of the nineteenth century.[25] This was further evidence of the stubborn persistence of deep-rooted beliefs that were impervious to scientific developments and another aspect of the unbelievably slow pace of change affecting the galenic framework in which pharmacology fused with dietetics. There was a constant toing and froing between retort and saucepan. Stag-antler jelly, which Francesco Redi also found tasty, was still being prescribed in the mid eighteenth century by the founder of pathological anatomy, Giovan Battista Morgagni. Like all Enlightenment doctors, Morgagni was a great believer in the miraculous properties of the irascible reptile and never tired of ordering it for his patients. It was served up to them either in soup form or as a liquid extract drawn from the retort. The combination of mountain viper with a little lean veal was served in the form of croquettes bound together with citron rinds in a preserve or, upon request, with a helping of balsam tips.[26]

'Chickens fed on viper meat'[27] were deemed to have 'reconstituent' properties, restoring natural heat and granting long life. However, the 'generous and potent white wine in which one deliberately would drown several live vipers',[28] even if in the eighteenth century it survived in special diets for the sick, no longer curried much favour with the healthy. In the second half of the eighteenth century the smell of the viper began to disappear from olfactory records. In part, the break with baroque culture was marked by the disappearance of this odour. From this point on there is no information whatever on diets wholly devoted to the viper or on the kind of obsessive eating habits that in the preceding century had not been all that unusual, as in the case of the

> virtuous and very noble gentleman, of a rather frail body, in the first bloom of his youth, who, during this summer [1664], during four weeks without interruption, drank every morning, at his breakfast, a dram of viperine powder diluted in a stock made from half of a viper, of the kind caught on the hills of Naples; for lunch, he ate a fine soup consisting of bread dipped in a viperine stock, salted and peppered (excuse the term) with viperine powder, and seasoned with the heart, liver and minced flesh of the same viper used in the stock; he drank wine in which vipers had been drowned; as an afternoon snack, he drank an emulsion prepared with a stock condensate and viper meat; in the evening he dined on the same kind of soup that he ate in the morning.[29]

It is hard to imagine what happened at the end of the four-week period strictly devoted to this charming reptile and whether the 'frail body' of the baronet was satisfactorily reinvigorated or not. Certainly it did him no harm. Indeed, there is no evidence at all in Redi's account to suggest even the slightest queasiness. Our curiosity on this score is doomed to remain unsated. However, apart from the account of this tireless consumer of viper meat, we have to conclude that, in general, 'chickens fed on viper meat' had an excellent flavour and that their taste was probably in no way inferior to today's variety, force-fattened at fixed intervals under blinding artificial light on fodder, the noblest ingredient of which consists of fish-meal.

It would appear, furthermore, that when cooked on a grill, vipers not only released a 'very suave fragrance'[30] but could stand comparison with grilled eel. There is an account of a septuagenarian who (we do not know whether from a desire for immortality or out of personal predilection) 'in the space of one month and a half ate more than ninety vipers caught in the summer and roasted in the way that cooks usually roast eels'.[31]

It is probably reasonable to believe, however, that viper meat encountered such widespread favour not least because of its fame as a means of preserving fading feminine beauty and above all because of its reputedly magical ability to bestow upon young women both grace and charm.

> I have not yet managed to establish whether the eating of these meats produces in the juvenile bodies of women (as some authors claim) that seemly proportion of parts and colours that one calls beauty, nor whether it restores to senile age its past beauty.[32]

If such an eminent investigator of nature's secrets as Redi failed to get to the bottom of this matter, it is pointless for us, however enthusiastic we may be as observers of the 'proportion of parts and colours' of feminine beauty, to try to resolve this age-old enigma.

SEVEN

EPHEMERAL DÉCOR

The jesters who during sixteenth- and seventeenth-century banquets 'kept everyone in festive mood with their pranks and witticisms'[1] had now all disappeared. Popular appreciation for 'coarse perfumes' was steadily declining. 'Fragrant balls full of live birds, with triumphant circles . . . made of magnificently and preciously scented pastries'[2] were obsolete, unknown. Banished too from luncheons and dinners were those waves of 'fragrant odours' that 'underneath the tables and for each table companion' in 'excessive copiousness'[3] had once stunned people with their dizzying outpourings. The Renaissance and the baroque were hurriedly quitting the eighteenth-century stage. The new, refined and delicate palate required a new nose, different smells, fragrances more intimate and muffled, more feminine aromas, gentler perfumes, breezy essences of plants. Pungent, animal and masculine smells, the civet, amber and musk that had hung heavy in the baroque atmosphere, were now rejected with disgust. From the earliest decades of the eighteenth century any 'woman of grace', on 'scenting amber', would pull

> a twisted mouth
> and say her womb is all inflamed.
> Another you can see that seems quite dead
> from tasting a musk-flavoured sweet
> and she will not come round till

filtered swilling piss –
sal volatile's the medical term –
is proffered to her dainty nose.[4]

Because of the fragile 'imagination of women and convulsionaries', a 'strong smell' could bring on 'odorous faintings'.[5] Delicate women, prone to palpitations and vapours and liable to fainting fits, would never go anywhere without their phials of essences, salts and spirits. Among women, the 'convulsive aura' became the most fashionable social disease, gradually taking the place of seventeenth-century hypochondria. Such sensitive and faddish creatures needed diets that were light, caressing, voluptuous, soft and sweet. Pastries, confectionery and buffet food enjoyed several years of unprecedented and unparalleled sophistication. The ban on 'heavy and viscous' meats was extended to cover any kind of 'strong-smelling food': cheese, cabbage, garlic, onion. One day in 1769 even a bunch of orange-flowers made Alessandro Verri feel 'nausea'.

The 'strong smell of citron in a cream paste' could bring on similar effects and some people came close to fainting just 'on the sight and smell of apples'.[6] Such a forceful rejection of acrid and violent smells and of over-emphatic tastes ('smell,' Alessandro Verri wrote, 'seems to me a taste, that is to say a flavour, that has been diminished')[7] bespoke the need to save the palate from the dulling effect of violent essences released by strong tastes as well as the desire to preserve it for 'more delicate pleasures' and sensations. But it also revealed the wish (or the need) to prevent particularly acrid stenches and base pongs from sending inconvenient olfactory messages likely to disturb those postprandial hours sacred to worldly conversation, to close encounters, to parlour games and, more generally, to the salon-world of relationships and gallantry wherein ladies played the starring prima donna roles. Discrimination against foods considered vulgar grew stronger and aristocratic snobbery more accentuated. Any survivals of the cross-class food habits of feudal society were now abolished root and branch. The diet of high society rose up to form yet another barrier against that other plebeian, populous and bourgeois world, one more device for clearly marking out the frontiers of privileged status. Disgust for particular social smells developed in parallel with the creation of the earliest rational and systematic campaigns for urban hygiene and deodorization. Borders separating different social environments seemed ever more clearly to entail a strict olfactory frontier.

Any 'social' history of the sense of smell that neglected food smells, that failed to poke its nose into kitchens, would risk slipping into the ideological abstraction of the sensualist *philosophes*. The much debated fortune of cheese, for example, belongs more to the history of smells than to the albeit parallel history of flavours. 'So far, too little has been done for the nose, whereas much too much has been done for the mouth . . . From smells to flavours there is but a small step,'[8] commented Cesare Beccaria as he pondered, light-heartedly, on the possibility of producing three folio volumes of *Elementa naseologiae methodo mathematica demonstrata* (Elements of the discipline of the sense of smell, based on mathematical methods). 'To cultivate one's body' while neglecting the 'pleasures of smell' appeared to Beccaria to be clear evidence of inexcusable barbarism. He noted with regret that

> the ancients were more partial to smells than we are, and those old Romans, whom other nations regarded as the masters of both virtues and pleasures, made a great use of fragrances at their banquets, in their baths and in their hypocausts. They used perfumes to caress and restore their bodies after sweating exercises in the gymnasia. Our antique furniture, which has kept its musky smell, shows us the good sense of our forefathers. But nowadays, to the mighty indignation of all men of good taste, for every hundred hairdressers, busy powdering and applying the most repugnant lard to the heads of this vast capital city, there are scarcely two perfumers at work comforting people's noses. And wherever my eyes alight I see nothing but open latrines, though no one ever thinks to remedy the stench that
>
> *Aequo pulsat pede pauperum tabernas*
> *Regumque turres.*
> [Comes out equally strong from the huts of the poor
> And the palaces of kings.]

Yet the pleasures afforded by the sense of smell are so innocent that, to my knowledge, no sect or religion has ever condemned them, nor among the strict communities of the Cœnobites do I see any that imposes vows of abstinence as regards smells . . . I would be very fortunate if I managed to convert these heretics of voluptuousness to the genial conversations and to the toilets of a lady.[9]

The strategy that aimed to eradicate the 'uncleanliness' and to 're-perfume air swamped by exhalations'[10] ran parallel to attempts at culinary reform made by society's elites. A determined effort was indeed being made to break with the culinary inheritance and to challenge the history, tradition, mental outlook and prejudices of the 'coarse centuries' and 'old times' (Muratori). The food codes adopted by Enlightenment culture reflected the accelerated pace of mental change in a fast-moving society determined to distance itself from the taste and culture of previous generations.

Taste, however, never evolves suddenly. Its development comes from afar and takes shape slowly, year on year, with the steady and unstoppable unravelling of time. In the final decades of the seventeenth century Tuscany experienced a substantial influx of French customs and fashions. In Florence Marquis Francesco Riccardi, who already had in his employ a 'French confectioner', in June 1690 recommended him to the Grand Duke, who, prudently, delayed engaging the confectioner, wishing first to test his abilities. Francesco Redi, who was not only a mediator between the court and the aristocracy and a skilful negotiator but also an unrivalled connoisseur of syrups and juleps, informed Marquis Riccardi that Cosimo III would appreciate it if

> his new confectioner would prepare him a small porcelain of those fruits in syrup called *compotes*, mentioned this morning, which His Highness would like to taste. He should, however, by no means provide anything else, for His Highness wishes to taste all the other good things that he knows how to prepare when, this summer, Your Most Illustrious Lordship gives his habitual and sumptuous picnic for the feast of St Margaret.[11]

Italy gradually adopted the 'service à la française', which had already been introduced into the Medici court of Cosimo III, the unfortunate consort of Marguerite Louise d'Orléans. The stand (*surtout*) was placed at the centre of the table, the *dessert* became an essential feature and the table setting (*couvert*) was increasingly personalized.

The taste of 'well-mannered' ladies demanded voluptuous consolations and a sophisticated arsenal of elegant utensils. Crystalware, fine porcelain, bowls, *sorbetières*, coffee-pots, cups, flasks, silverware and enamelware, little boxes and saucers all entered into the new rituals that surrounded the taking of coffee, tea, chocolate, sorbets, rosolios, lozenges and coloured pastilles, powders, biscuits and petits fours, finger biscuits, compotes, rose and violet conserves, little buns, *clairettes* (a 'kind of transparent fruit paste that might be better termed dry jellies even though they were still served like those natural jellies that come in small glass jars, and are served in small tumblers, glasses or in boxes lined with fine paper'),[12] icings and frostings, candied fruit, marzipan, mousses, meringues, *pignoccate* (sweet cakes containing pine seeds), wafers, iced buns, iced and pearled ring-shaped cakes, dry, liquid and royal conserves, sugared almonds (small and large chocolate-filled sweets, *diavoletti* and *diavoloni*), 'grigliaggi', little pearls, candied flowers, artificial flowers and fruit ('sugared nets of citron'), 'iced jasmines, violets, hyacinths and daffodils', sweets, honey milk, spiced puddings (*bombe*) with fruit and honey, meringues, creams, very delicate syrups like so-called maidenhair syrup, or 'daffodil crushed-ice drinks' (*granitas*).

At a time when cuisine was making up in sophistication and elegance what it was losing in abundance and opulence the look of food acquired key importance: it had to be apparent at a single glance that the meal on offer was of top quality. The trend towards refinement in table service and the graceful miniaturization of dining utensils, along with the vogue for informal and confidential meetings (*petits soupers*), found expression in a number of different ways: increasingly minute tableware and crockery (plates often reduced to saucer size); strongly personalized table places (*couverts*); the centre-of-table display (*surtout*), devoted to a variety of subjects but with a clear preference for temples made of *massé* sugar (cooked at 125 degrees centigrade and shaped using a spatula); the scenographic *dessert* built on top of a broad base *en pastillage* ('a mixture of gum tragacanth, of glacé sugar, starch and lemon'); and, lastly, the vases of flowers modelled out of almond paste. *Ephemeral decorations*, fleeting masterworks of decorative art created by brilliant and inventive master pastry-chefs who had to combine the skills of painters, draughtsmen, fashion designers, architects, sculptors and florists. Often these monumental compositions, these arabesqued tableaux, took 400 hours to construct and used up a hundredweight of sugar and 15 kilos of almond paste. Also needed were gifted artists, whimsical inventors of 'edifices', English-style parks, French-type gardens, statues, vases, water fountains fed by cleverly concealed hydraulic machinery, tableaux showing the passage of the four seasons, alternating on a base like the movements of a symphony, from a wintry landscape (at the beginning of the meal) to a spring scene, thence to summer, in line with the mounting heat of the food, then melting away slowly, turning to liquid, vanishing altogether.

Sugary concerts that could be seen and heard, fading away with the notes of a string orchestra, trembling and tumbling like music on the water.

It was a triumph for the art of the buffet, 'where taste reigns just as supreme' as 'refinement and the sense of smell. It forms the most beautiful of sights,' wrote the greatest practitioner and theoretician of this refined offshoot of cookery 'of a table properly laid.' 'After the dishes themselves,' Francesco Leonardi continued, the art of the buffet 'provides delight, distraction and recreation at a magnificent and sumptuous table.'[13]

As Leonardi remarked in 1807, 'over the last few years this art in Italy has made the most rapid of progress and it might soon reach absolute perfection thanks to the genius, talent and fertile imagination of the artists involved'.[14]

> I am not talking of work using oven or casserole for, as far as that is concerned, the French have left us far behind and we have just tried to improve our work by imitating them. But this is really no more than a straightforward restitution since, two centuries and a half earlier, it was from us that they received their first ideas on

good taste and on delicacy in the matter of serving at table . . . The French, who are, besides, full of genius, talent, skill and are of a lively and quick imagination, have surpassed us not only in the art of cookery and to a considerable extent in the art of the buffet, but also in many other brilliant sciences and arts that form and will ever continue to be the glory of the French nation.[15]

The acknowledgement of French superiority and hegemony in matters of 'good taste' and in the 'delicacy' of their culinary science was accompanied by a proud awareness that 'this art in Italy has made the most rapid of progress'.[16]

> One only has to observe the *composition of fine table liqueurs*, which have now reached such a degree of excellence that they could only with difficulty be surpassed, and also the *manipulation and the variation of iced sorbets*. Here are two luxury articles, of a delicacy and taste of which one can boast throughout the length and breadth of Europe. *Italian liqueurs* and *Italian-style ice-cream* are phrases spoken by peoples of all foreign nations. Tuscany is renowned for its *liquori*, Naples for its *gelati*. And yet in Rome, Bologna and Turin there are manufacturers of liqueurs who are just as good as those of Florence and Leghorn. The same may be said for ice-creams. Similarly, in Rome and in Milan there are artists whom, thanks to the precise and well-designed taste of their iced sorbets, many consider to be superior to the Neapolitans, whom they criticize for using too much sugar.[17]

Lined up on the buffet, alongside the sweets and the sorbets, were table liqueurs, the pride of Italian spicery, from which modern liquor distillery is derived. These, as the modern Apicius wrote, were divided into four main categories:

> liqueurs made by *distillation*, liqueurs made by *infusion* and *distillation* and liqueurs made with *filtered fruit juices*. The fourth of these categories includes both *rosolios* and *ratafias* also. All of these liqueurs may be either simple or compound – made of several different ingredients. Rosolios and ratafias may be defined as sweet and aromatized liqueurs, made to satisfy taste and smell . . .

The composition of fine table liqueurs depends to an enormous degree on the talent and good taste of the individual artist. The artist may, after all, carry out a good number of experiments on each idea that presents itself to his imagination. He may mix several liqueurs together and so arrive at some happy combinations. These combinations may be able to throw much light on the physics of smells and flavours and help to discover new liqueurs capable of satisfying the desires of voluptuous and sophisticated people. Such theoretical matters would lead me into over-lengthy details. I shall therefore limit myself to laying out a methodical and experimental plan that one might put into practice in this area of table luxury and pleasure.[18]

Thus, while placing the 'light' generated by the 'physics of smells and flavours' at the disposal of the 'voluptuous and sophisticated', Leonardi, that tireless guide to cookery and the buffet and the author of the novelistic introduction to *Gianina ossia La Cuciniera delle Alpi* (1817), somehow found time, between one sitting and the next, to fill eleven volumes with recipes. Moreover, throwing open his scintillating pantry to the devotees of luxury and pleasure (the keywords of eighteenth-century hedonism and profane moral philosophy), he exhibited forty-six varieties of rosolios, twenty-two types of ratafia, thirty-eight kinds of syrup, seventy-two sorts of drinks or beverages, 'some vinegary, others milky, yet others the straightforward fruits or flowers that one serves when the weather is hot... infinitely refreshing and quenching'; and yet others, like 'lemonade, the bitter juice of the citron, orangeade, crushed-ice drinks, acetous syrup, oxymel, oxycrate, etc., if they are diluted with lots of fresh water or chilled with snow, except in the case of oxycrate, have a powerfully calming effect on putrid, malign and inflammatory fevers'.[19]

EIGHT

A BLISSFUL AND DRINKABLE ETERNITY

Urns of sweetly scented snow, caskets of 'frozen humours' and 'icy treasures', *sorbetières*, whether silver or gold plated, had for many years been an instrument of 'icy delights'.[1] Throughout endless summer droughts, on scorching summer days, the *sorbetière* would suddenly appear, speckled with frost, a comforting sight that promised 'a thousand various sweetnesses'. Chocolate sorbet turned into a 'holy and noble elixir of fresh life' as it slipped down one's throat.[2] Embellished with vanilla, orange zest and drops of distilled jasmine, chocolate 'in garapegra' as Italians called it, using the Spanish term, iced chocolate consoled the spirits, brought relief to blood that had almost curdled and clotted in the pit of overheated lungs, inflamed by the implacable breath of August, that 'distiller of living flesh'.

> On a triumphal coffin
> Strewn with flowers and herbs
> Raise that icy
> Stove aloft:
> That massive silver
> Cradles in its icy heart
> Alive and fresh
> An autumn-full of sorbets.[3]

For the pleasure of gallant snacks and the 'joy of dinners', the 'miracle of ice-cream' summoned from the 'noble abyss'

A BLISSFUL AND DRINKABLE ETERNITY 73

> Foam, snow and life-giving hail,
> Snow-white milk drinks,
> Flavoured with violets.
> And that proud chocolate,
> The terror of raw winter,
> Now, thanks to rough handling,
> Is turned into summer's treat.[4]

On 'ardent days', the 'frozen western manna' would prise open precious chinks, would spark sweetly scented ecstasies that could feed on its composite, exotic fragrance, its 'sprinkling of a twofold smell': vanilla ('of Indian cultivations / The most fragrant of daughters') and the 'strong-smelling zest' of the 'distinguished orange', 'of which Tuscany strives to grow rich'.[5]

> On raising to your lips
> The rich and mystical drink
> What fragrancy, my Nise!
> Noble, ineffable, admirable,
> A fragrance for the soul.
> 'Tis a smell, 'tis food, life, glory, luck,
> The perennial luck, the everlasting
> Fresh, suave, limpid and serene luck
> Of a blissful and drinkable eternity.[6]

The 'blissful and drinkable eternity' that sent Count Magalotti into such transports was in fact the sweet cocoa-tinged elixir that 'this blessed New World'[7] had donated to old Europe in order to soften and refine tastebuds that had grown accustomed over centuries to pungent drugs from the Levant. It was a providential liquid that the barbarous West injected into the veins of voluptuous Europeans.

> As soon as you have drunk it down
> Into your stomach in generous gulps
> This pearl
> This jewel
> This beautiful American julep;

Scarcely is it sloshing inside you
This western manna
But it washes you and cleanses you
Of every bitter and mortal worry.
And while it circulates around
Winding through your arteries and veins,
Mingling and fused in that vermilion sauce
That, through its action, flows fine and free,
Who now remembers the sun or scorching heat?[8]

The new Mexican treasure gushed forth from its inexhaustible horn of plenty heavenly and outlandish powders and dreamy juleps: delicacies from the tropics. From 'Indian cultures', from Pernambuco and from Baya, from Panama and from Santa Fe, from Soconosco and from Carthage, from Brazil, from Guatemala and from Mexico, there arrived untried marvels which, when combined with equally unknown substances from the Orient, formed a 'twin treasure'. From India 'divine eagle-wood', sandalwood, cinnamon; from the Far East, tea and catechu; from the West, vanilla, 'Peru rubber', balsam from Tolù, quinine (aromatic cinchona), but above all 'precious bitumen', 'Indian magistery, by which the palate / Summer and winter is blessed', black chocolate, 'which is sifted on the bank of the Tagus / By the vestal at Santa Chiara / Great powder'; the 'deep black dust' whose preparation required 'grains of musk in cartloads, / Sheets of bezoar by the ounce, / Black balsam in bucketfuls, / Ambergris by the ton'.

You feel running through your veins
The rush of wind from a fan and bellows,
As if the Zephyr hard was blowing
Fully throated through your lips:
As if its breath was bringing you
All the western drugs from sunrise:
Balsam, bezoar and, melted, drenched,
Several tears of rich quinquina:
Soconosco, Guatemala's source of wealth.
And also, as if it has attracted,
Through the power of its breathing,

Not western fragrances alone
But in an instant each and every
Perfume of the Orient,
The rivers of the mosques and harems
And all is fetched to noble lungs
As to a precious gold alembic,
And in a fresh new style's distilled,
The twinning treasure of East and West.[9]

In this great witches' sabbath of aromas criss-crossing from East and West, in this late-baroque joust of the senses ('Treasures from the Molucca Islands, Arab odours', as the old Florentine dandy wrote in *La donna immaginaria*), 'perfumer sprites'[10] danced their last mad saraband. 'Good bread, good wine, good fruit, good air, these things, said Grand Duke Ferdinand, are the treasures of our temperate countries: silver, gold, pearls and other such joys, these are the prerogatives of torrid climes ... Playfulness, gracefulness, kindness, health and recreation: these are the strengths of our European lands. Nobility, wealth, strong aromas, majesty, vagueness, vitality, marvels, these belong to the lands of America.'[11]

Everything that was native, everything cultivated in the gardens, kitchen gardens and fields of Italy or that grew there of its own accord, seemed to have lost the power to attract.

It is worth a treasure
It is worth all Peru,
If it comes from Mogor,
If it comes from Tolù.[12]

Even the rose had fallen into dark disgrace. Under a drooping sun, it continued pointlessly to flower. Its scent now seemed common, old-fashioned, slightly vulgar. Its ancient and emblematic charm seemed to have faded:

Because it grows in their own country
Nobody any longer deigns to caress it,
Everyone shows contempt;
Princes and marquises

Its perfume deem a stink
Unless it smell of distant places.[13]

It seemed to be the shared fate of ephemeral flowers to experience a blazing and lightening dawn followed by the melancholy of equally sudden sunsets. France, which in the middle of the seventeenth century discovered the wonders of maidenhair fern, by the eighteenth century had forgotten it in favour of the exotic *Calycanthus floridus*. This flower was renamed 'le Pompadour', the name acquired by an obscure and casual woman of the people who had used the flower as a magic olfactory talisman in order to seduce the King of France. Marie Antoinette, somewhat less fortunate, launched a fashion in high Versailles society for the potato flower, but this proved very short-lived. The same thing occurred with the tuberose.

In Italy a similar fate befell jasmine, dislodged from favour by the honeysuckle. Italian jasmine was abandoned, overwhelmed by Catalonian jasmine, of which the rare variety known as Gimè was particularly appreciated. But no Catalonian jasmine could compete with Indian jasmine, *Jasminum sambac*, also known as 'Mogorium goaense'. It was in fact from Goa that one fine day in 1688 there arrived at Palazzo Pitti, by way of Portugal, a gift from the Portuguese monarch that was designed to console the hypochondriac Cosimo for the loss of various plants that a Chieti-born monk had previously tried to send him but which had sunk along with the ship that was carrying them. Cosimo conceived such a passion for the Indian jasmine that when at last he received it he had it jealously guarded in his Castello villa and categorically forbade anyone from taking grafts, bedding it out or layering it. The exclusive love borne this shrub by the lord of Etruria – who, according to the ambassadors accredited to Palazzo Pitti, 'had little appetite for the consort'[14] and 'is never seen to laugh'[15] – earned it the nickname 'the Grand Duke's jasmine'. For more than a century this extremely rare little plant could not even be touched and it was not until the end of the eighteenth century that Pietro Leopoldo began to allow cuttings to be taken. Yet Magalotti managed at last to send to Queen Anne of England a sample of this incomparably fragrant plant ('the breath of your breast / Is poison / To the glory of every flower').[16] To avoid outraging the morbid passion that Cosimo felt for the 'double jasmine from Goa called jasmine of the heart', it had to be sent dried.

This enemy of vice, a prince of 'wondrous continence',[17] an impassioned student of cosmography, geometry (like all the late Medicis), botany, citrus cultivation and pomology, who was merely prone 'to eating too abundantly',[18] 'sombre' because he suffered from 'melancholic affection',[19] dedicated to continuous exercises of devotion, to 'penitence and abstinence'[20] (the 'slight intemperance as regards food'[21] was but an insignificant weakness, a necessary surrogate for the lack of wifely affection), fell head over heels in love with a flower. He hated his wife, the beautiful, vivacious, effervescent Marguerite Louise d'Orléans, niece of the Sun King, 'all gallantry',[22] who being unwilling to renounce 'living in French style'[23] took great pleasure 'in songs, dances and hunts'.[24] The 'most serene bride', who in her not very frequent moments of desperation considered 'shutting herself away in France in a convent' rather than 'reigning in Florence with the Grand Duke',[25] consoled herself as best she might, 'but, above all, by organizing afternoon treats'.[26] These 'merende', generally held on grass lawns, had come into being in the seventeenth century but became one of the central features of eighteenth-century gallant life, on a par with 'petits soupers' and country fêtes in a world beautified by Arcadian pastoral poetry.

For such snacks nothing could be better than an omelette. In Tuscany the favourite kind of omelette contained distinctly un-Arcadian 'pips': the testicles of lambs or of other less lovable and docile quadrupeds. In 'La merenda', a mature work, Magalotti – having progressed from the Accademia del Cimento to the Accademia della Crusca and thence to the Accademia dell'Arcadia – asked the 'shepherdess' Nise to 'relieve his hunger' by frying in lard a nice panful of testicles: 'of a thousand lambs so as to assuage your hunger / Killed in their infancy in a copper bowl / The abortive pips of a fried herd'.[27] But it seems that the Count was exaggerating. In 1694 he complained in a letter to Leone Strozzi that 'the pips and the omelettes in this season's snacks ... when they appear on the table, are not looked upon with respect'.[28] If the 'Most serene Mistress' had deigned to repair to his 'vegetable garden' to partake of his snack, he would have taken care not to offer her (as his manservant might have liked to offer certain ladies) a 'panlavato di cacciù' (that is, slices of toasted bread dipped in water and seasoned with a sauce of mimosa catechu). He would rather have presented her with an omelette made with fresh eggs (the classical thin Florentine-style omelette), some 'good Casentino ham' and, by way of gallantry, a 'panlavato' with 'good muscatel, a plentiful sprinkling of sugar and plenty of ice underneath'.[29] It would have been like 'throwing away a gift' to give certain people (albeit of quality and high rank) delicacies that only great voluptuaries, with perfectly educated noses, were able to appreciate. A waste of refinement to set to boil 'at the bottom of a Maya *bucchero*, with water of Cordoba, four or six shards of Guadalajara *bucchero* kept an entire year in an amber-scented skin so that they might soak up its fragrance, along with a fraction of a droplet of quinine'. Since 'for these people, the greatest gift does not consist in the smell itself' but 'in doing them the honour of showing them that you believe they take pleasure in smells',[30] any old hotchpotch will do: 'as far as they are concerned, everything is good'. Rather than wasting rare and costly ingredients it made better sense to prepare for 'these domestic Tartars' something slightly less sublime, falling back on a cheap recipe: 'the rind of a used-up orange, a bit of pounded benzoin, a couple of crushed carnations, a stick of cinnamon; cover the lot with plenty of rose water, and set it to boil on the brazier'.[31] For a tête-à-tête on the lawn, a fragrant omelette of orange-flowers would be the ideal dish, quite tasty and easy to prepare, cheap, straightforward yet captivating. In no way vulgar.

> What shall we make? I seem to recall
> A way of making an omelette –
> Not bad at all, if I remember correctly:
> Listen, Nise, you will thank me for it.
> The recipe is easily told
> And not much expense is incurred,

Eggs, butter, salt and some heat:
It's a matter as quick as it's simple.
There is not all that much
That is unusual about it:
And though I'm not blinded by Love
It seems quite appealing to me.
After thoroughly beating the eggs,
In the best and professional way,
Add to the frying-pan
Morsels of orange-flower
Specially kept for the purpose.[32]

But any truly gallant snack must feature not only 'Canary Island or Tersera amber', 'Hungarian Tokay', Frontignac and 'that fruity Bacharach wine' but also sorbets. In the countryside, 'when it is cool / just the two of us, / we shall have a light but noble snack. / Beneath a Turkey oak, / so vastly huge, / one feels quite lost, / on a boulder covered / by a green, green moss', on which, as on a throne, a

large and golden *sorbetière*,
proud and so majestic,
stands right in the middle,
its outside covered in mist.[33]

When the lady opened the *sorbetière*, she would discover

Four pounds of succulent strawberries
As massive as walnuts or bigger,
Washed in amber water and a rosolio
Of the most fragrant that ever there was;
Then soaked at the moment of daybreak
In a glass of milk, and thereupon laid
In a pot-pourri that the very Sofi
Would pay a vast treasure to own.[34]

Whether for the 'fun of the hunt' or to provide a 'dinner gift',[35] several new animal species had been introduced into Italy, swelling existing princely reserves. In 1683 Magalotti wrote to his imaginary 'atheist' correspondent as follows:

In my time, I have seen arriving in Tuscany white peacocks, white pheasants, guinea-fowl, Corsican partridges and hazel-grouse. In the case of the grouse, thirty years ago one could find none at all or only very few in any single reserve, whereas today there are many reserves stocked principally with such game. The same may be said as regards white deer and black deer, grey rabbits and black rabbits.[36]

To provide a ladies' pastime and to assuage feminine listlessness, 'speckled dogs from Poland and many other odd new crossbreeds of lapdogs were introduced, as I believe, into nature itself'.[37] The term 'svogliatura' (rendered here as 'listlessness') had gained broad currency among the post-Galileo generation. Evangelista Torricelli spoke of 'listlessness' and of 'listless Europe' long before Magalotti turned his attention to spiritual languor and to the 'listlessness and hypochondria of greed'. In Magalotti's view such 'listless modern gluttony' became more widespread at times when the crisis of European consciousness began to impinge on cookery, ancient appetites and post-Renaissance taste.

The plantations of America and, in particular, the islands of the Caribbean, dispatched great quantities of those sugars that 'the English have so prodigiously multiplied on the islands of Jamaica, Barbados, Nevis, St Christopher, Antigua, Montserrat'.[38] During the eighteenth century, thanks to the constant supply of cane-sugar and the new cost-cutting shipping route, sugar began to replace honey and figs, an increasing number of hymns were composed to sugar and the art of sugar refinery reached its apogee. The 'many foreign flowers and fruits' that arrived from the New World and of which, as Magalotti observed in 1683, 'we see that our Italy is now full',[39] began to be cultivated in greenhouses and gardens. This influx of new essences coincided with the art of plant grafts developed by the 'admirable melancholy of florists and gentleman farmers'.[40] This was particularly apparent in Medicean Tuscany where the grand dukes and princes were often also 'natural philosophers', passionate observers of the natural order and eager hunters after wondrous plants. The ancient 'art of making grafts',[41] 'a true manufacture of art',[42] often managed to bring into being eccentric botanical freaks, 'plants of weirdness', 'the prize and astonishment of Etruscan gardens',[43] where it was hard to clarify to what extent they were the 'true and legitimate offspring of nature' and not rather a hybrid and deviant progeny 'conceived... in adultery by human artifice'.[44] In 1640 uncertainty was aroused by the birth of the *cedrarancio* (a cross between a lemon and an orange), which appeared without warning one day in the suburban garden of Torre degli Agli, a property belonging to the strange Florentine canon and exemplary member of the Accademia della Crusca, Lorenzo Panciatichi. In the summer of 1676 Panciatichi, an author of dithyrambic verse and an intimate of Magalotti, fell victim to melancholy and ended his days by hurling himself into a well. It was no easy thing to determine the exact paternity of the *cedrarancio*, this 'hermaphrodite fruit',[45] half lemon and half orange. Carlo Roberto Dati, who described the event in both verse and prose, wondered whether that 'vague monster'[46] was 'a whim of art or of nature or, to put it better, of luck'.[47] However, Magalotti, a friend of both Dati and Panciatichi, was in no doubt that it had been the gardener who had assembled 'either the seeds or the grafts of the orange, lemon and citron, so that a shoot would arise capable of producing all three fruits separately and then a fruit combining the features of all three'.[48]

A taste for rarity, for strangeness, for the freak that overstepped the bounds of nature's geometrical order prompted collectors to depict on canvas the aberrant offspring that *vis genitiva* (the regenerative power of nature), through its own mysterious and deviant processes, brought into the world. Ever since the reign of Cosimo I generation after generation of painters specializing in the depiction of flowers and fruits had painted both the riches of the Tuscan Pomona and the unchecked oddities that astounded the eyes of gentleman flower-growers and farmers. At the time of Prince Leopold, while Magalotti was engaged as the Medicis' supervisor at the 'museum of natural things', the Prince himself had required him to observe and describe with close, almost morbid, attention the respiration of the night, the odorous breathing and 'wonderful extravagance' of the *Pelargonium triste, sive indicum* (Sorrowful pelargonium, otherwise known as Indian pelargonium). Magalotti's own house in Florence was crammed full of drawings and paintings of natural subjects (including fish and 'shells'). On searching through some old cupboards in 1704 Magalotti, by this time advanced in years, stumbled upon paintings that he had forgotten. As he wrote to Leone Strozzi, a collector of *buccheri*, shells, all kinds of rare objects and porcelains (the Medicis had sought to reproduce Chinese porcelains, though with disappointing results):

> while rummaging through my cupboards, my eyes were drawn by certain unusual paintings of flowers and fruits: for example, a hyacinth with 136 little bells, which Cardinal Giovanni Carlo had in his garden in Via de la Scala; a famous carnation originating from Flanders, as big as a peony, and fresh too; a double or quadruple jasmine flower, which had appeared two years earlier in the Castello garden, bearing more than 300 leaves; an apricot that grew this year in the Vagaloggia orchard, and weighed more than 5 ounces and 10 deniers; and, lastly, a jasmine of Catalonia that bloomed last month in the Magalotti Gardens, and boasted more than 17 leaves. Tell me if, of all these rarities, there is any that would please you.[49]

NINE

THE BOTANY OF THE PALATE

While coffee and chocolate became the liquid emblem of a new society that was pulling in two directions – highly-strung yet lazy, keen yet listless, industrious yet hedonistic, a late sleeper yet an early riser – orangeade and lemonade also enjoyed a prominent place on Enlightenment tables. These soft drinks were combined with a 'botany of the palate'[1] whereby 'all the most tasty herbs and fruits from Asia, Africa and America, asparagus, melons, and the most exquisite lettuces from Holland' served as side dishes for 'grapes of Good Hope' and the 'distinguished lineage of pineapples'.[2] In the years straddling the seventeenth and eighteenth centuries Holland imported from both the East and the Caribbean an unprecedented range of goods previously unknown to the old economic and dietary order. While the tulip somehow came to symbolize Dutch mercantile industriousness (in competition with the English East India Company), the new hybrid vegetables, the latest fruit and grapes and the new herbs that lent themselves to unheard-of infusions made their entry into the aristocratic and bourgeois world of Europe and Italy. In 1705 Lorenzo Magalotti wrote to Leone Strozzi:

> Today I went to visit a lady who has only recently arrived here from Holland. Without mentioning the world of extremely select porcelains that I saw, I shall tell you only of a rarity that she did me the great honour of presenting and that I am sure will seem as new

to you as it did to us. In short, she served me with Bu tea. 'Bu' must be an Indian word. Its true meaning is not known. It is known, however, that it is the distinctive name for a particular species of tea that arrived three hundred years ago from the same region from which the other tea also came. Its leaf, which verges on the black, is shrivelled like green tea. But when it has been soaked and spread out, it is notably much larger than the green leaf. It is prepared in exactly the same way. The difference lies in the fact that whereas green tea, when it is poured into a bowl, shows a rather yellowish colour, Bu tea produces a rosy colour, and its fragrance and taste also recall roses, just as green tea recalls violets. Bu tea is also considered more diuretic than the green variety. As regards the preparation of green tea, the fashion nowadays is no longer to put the sugar in the bowl but instead to place in one's mouth a lump of candied sugar. One then drinks the boiling tea over this lump, melting it a little at each mouthful, so that the tea is rendered syrupy as one drinks it. With Bu tea, however, as it is somewhat more austere, one places the sugar in the bowl to melt.[3]

Dutch sugar loaves had no serious competition, not even in Venice. From Holland there arrived unknown essences that the 'Italian voluptuary', a lover of 'mysterious ices made from flowers and fruits, served in his golden *sorbetières*',[4] analysed with scientific precision and sophisticated erudition. In October 1705 Magalotti wrote to Strozzi to inform him that

> the evening before last His Most Serene Prince of Tuscany did me the honour of presenting me with two liqueurs that, as far as I know, are not found here in Italy, and that His Highness had recently received from Holland, brought there on the latest Batavian boats. The gifts consist of two small carafes of essences, both of which can be recognized as citrus essences: one of fruit only, the other of flowers, and most probably of leaves, or rather of their tips or 'summits' – to adopt the term used in Rome. In the fruit carafe one can smell all the pride of the sulphur of the green rind of the rose-apple, but so pungent that at the first whiff you might think you were smelling carob, but then, considered more coolly, you discover without any doubt the smell of citrus and, amidst the citrus, the sharpness, as I was saying, of the rose-apple,

which in colour verges on the white. The other one, yellower and lighter, is also sweeter and has precisely that smell which remains on your fingers when you have just crushed the tips of citron or of lime.[5]

Extraordinary expertise was needed to find a way through such a maze of vegetation, and great sensory subtlety was essential to recognize through taste and smell the full range of messages emitted by classical and exotic botany. The art and inventive skills invested in the planning and creation of hybrids, graftings and new varieties were nurtured during the lengthy periods that the most sophisticated of aristocrats now dedicated to their gardens, hothouses and open-air studies.

The garden planted by Count Pietro Verri was divided into two sections, one 'wholly in accordance with the French taste for the parterre' and the other of English design, dominated by untamable 'fierce nature', free from any geometrical plan.[6] In this garden and in its 'carefully heated greenhouses' 'the most exotic and strange of fruits'[7] were cultivated and 'at the end of autumn' 'peaches, cherries and many other spring and summer gifts' could be gathered.[8] Only two generations after Magalotti a rising tide of exoticism and cosmopolitanism had already pushed to one side the calculated symmetry of the Italian garden, which had long symbolized the harmony of the world and provided a heavenly image of the divine cloister. In these heated greenhouses and redesigned gardens even pineapples were cultivated. Francesco Leonardi, cosmopolitan cook and latter-day Apicius of mixed heritage (Italy and St Petersburg), recommended a jelly made from pineapple that 'could be used to make iced sorbets and jelly desserts, when fresh fruit is unavailable'.[9] In 1760, as he roamed around the deserted Portuguese countryside, among fields of 'the most delicate-smelling rosemary', Giuseppe Baretti wrote to his brothers that 'of all exotic plants . . . I only know and love the pineapple, fruit of the tropics, which I have heard is now being introduced into many parts of Italy'.[10]

The scent of the pineapple was considered 'pleasing' and its 'delicious flavour' very special 'inasmuch as it combines different tastes together'. Owing to their 'exquisiteness', pineapples became essential items on 'the most sumptuous tables, where they are both decoration and delicacy'.[11] Pineapples were considered so exquisite and pleasing that their entrance into the temple of eighteenth-century taste was irresistible. At first they were imported from the tropics, but they were later cultivated in 'stoves' or hothouses in Lombardy, Tuscany, Rome and other regions. This new crop spread far and wide. 'Especially in Italy,' Francesco Leonardi recalled, 'there are excellent plantations in stoves. In Rome pineapples are to be found in the garden of the Quirinale, in the Vatican's "Indian Garden" and in the charming Villa Pinciana. It may therefore be said that this delightful fruit is no longer so very rare.'[12] From Paris to Berlin 'the yellow pineapple', born 'of a counterfeit summer', generously distributed the 'misappropriated treasure of its fruit'.[13] At Potsdam, in the gardens of the Sans-Souci palace, 'created, as it were, by this king with the art of Armida',[14] pineapples ripened for the pleasure of Frederick and his extraordinary guests. In 1751 Francesco Algarotti wrote a letter saying:

> This climate is not so far from the path of the sun to stop it competing in almost every detail with better climates: and where nature has not been quite so benign, art and study compensate for it. And do not believe too readily that, as was said of Warsaw by one of our fine minds:
>
> *A lemon from Naples would be such a prize*
> *That if the King could possess it*
> *He would embed it in the royal diadem.*
>
> You can eat here too such excellent peaches, fine melons and figs that are sometimes in no way inferior to our own Italian ones with their long twisted necks and burst skins. The pineapple, this manna, this king of fruits, has become almost common here.[15]

At the 'dinners of the King', in those same days, Algarotti was able to enjoy the 'rare mind of Monsieur de Voltaire',[16] a man who, according to Abbot Bettinelli, 'took a great deal of coffee after draining his bottles'.[17]

The 'kingly' fruits were cut into rings and 'sprinkled with Spanish wine and sugar or with eau-de-vie and lots of sugar or with rosolios and sugar'.[18] A manna fit for princes, pineapples were also eaten 'baked in white wine and then candied like quinces . . . With pineapples,' Leonardi continued, 'you can make two kinds of compote, one kind of conserve, a variety of little buns, cakes, a jelly and an iced sorbet.'[19] And, last but not least, a 'dessert jelly, to use when there is no fresh fruit'.

The new exoticisms all looked eastwards, towards the Land of the Rising Sun and above all towards that enigmatic country China. In 1769 a 'Chinese fair' was held in Parma, with 'Chinese-type clothes'.[20] Private homes were suddenly invaded by Chinese porcelains, and elegant salons papered with silks, *boiseries* and 'painted papers'. But not without eliciting cautious reservations from such connoisseurs as Algarotti.

> The mediocrity of the Chinese, as in so many other things, is clearly manifest in their painting. Anyone who would talk of a diversity of Chinese schools or Chinese styles would be mistaken. All their figurines or pagodas are part of a single family: and one might indeed say that this countless nation has never had but one eye with which to see objects and but one hand with which to represent them.[21]

It is hard to imagine that this sophisticated companion of Frederick II and admirer of the poet Parini was in the habit of slipping his languid body into a 'silk cymar bearing a leafy Chinese design' in the guise of a dressing-gown.

Following the enormous European success that greeted the Baron de Montesquieu's *Lettres persanes*, Persia also insinuated itself into the culinary and other dreams of certain Italian nobles. In Milan the Count of Somaglia regularly 'ordered Persian dishes to be prepared, following the recipes of Jean Chardin [the great Parisian-born explorer of Persia, 1643–1713], and these dishes turned out to be good'.[22]

The internationalism of food and the cosmopolitanism of taste were particularly pronounced in the merry battle of wines between the 'joyful liqueurs of the hills of France / or of Spain or of Tuscany, or the Hungarian / bottle to which Bacchus awarded the crown / of green ivy, and said: "Be seated, / queen of the tables"'.[23] In this colourful contest between sweet-smelling drinks, held against a fast-moving and multi-faceted oenological background, it was the Italian wines that took the worst beating. The 'Hungarian bottle', Tokay, swept the board. In 1750, writing from Potsdam to F. Maria Zanotti, Algarotti commented:

> Water is indeed an excellent thing, and I drink plenty of it. Yet I do not fail to blend it with the divine drink of Homer, who, as you know, here [at the court of Frederick the Great] enjoys a much greater vogue than does Pindar . . . The first glass is for myself, as Sir Temple used to say, the second is for my friends, the third for joy, the fourth for my enemies . . . But when I drink the fourth or the fifth glass for my enemies, I give them the pleasure of drinking Tokay. Oh, that wine, my dear Mister Francesco! And if only our dear Redi had tasted of it, especially the outstanding vintages of 1715 and 1726, he would have changed his opinion and would not have declared, I am quite sure, that
>
> *Montepulciano is the king of all wines.*[24]

Fine wines arrived in Italy from all directions: Germany, Austria, the Tyrol; malmseys from the Canaries and muscat from Madeira; white wines from the Lebanon, Cyprus, Smyrna and red wines from Samos; wines both red and white from Scopoli (an island in the Euxine sea); Hungarian white wines (St George, 'Sciumelao', Razestoff) and Hungarian red wines (Erlau, Vaxen). And, of course, French, Spanish and Portuguese wines. Both red and white wines reached Italian tables even from the Cape of Good Hope. Wines from southern Africa did battle with wines from the plains of the Danube amid the bewildered scepticism and indignation of the scholars of old Italy, that ancient and mythical Oenotria. From his secluded and glorious northern city of Ferrara, Girolamo Baruffaldi had his 'Bacco in Giovecca' inveigh against the 'over-bodied and barbarous Tokay, / That stains your lips but never slakes your thirst'.[25]

From Bassano, G. B. Roberti recalled with just a hint of bitterness (in his old man's style) Italy's former supremacy as the land of wine.

> All meals that have any solemnity about them are customarily embellished by wine from overseas or from beyond the Alps. Wine from the Cape of Good Hope and Tokay, considered to be among the best in the world, are not unknown among us. Italian flasks are now deemed only barely sufficient; and yet the same Italy, with its wine harvests, has produced among other famous wines, the great Opimianum.[26]

Wines from Hungary, from southern Africa, all those wines that had crossed 'the seas and the Alps', the strange and peculiar bottles that arrived from faraway places, added a certain exotic sophistication to the prestige of cosmopolitan tables. Thrown on to the defensive as regards its wines, when it came to solid foods, Italian tradition was also losing ground. Those foreign 'opaque bottles' of the golden world of Roberti's 'La moda' had swept Italian flasks from elegant tables. The Count and Abbot of Bassano, a man well attuned to the latest shifts and trends in taste, acknowledged current preferences and alterations; but he also assessed with care the resistance that individual provinces and the tradition of Italy as a whole were able to rally in an effort to withstand the apparently ineluctable advance of eating habits and snobbish affectations that were then flooding into Italy wholesale and higgledy-piggledy. On St Martin's Day in 1780, in a letter he sent from a village in the Veneto to Gian Lodovico Bianconi, Roberti wrote that

> the wine of Lombardy is a healthy and full-bodied table wine. Ours is equally healthy, but it is more pungent for party purposes and more generous for fooling around... Almost every noble family has its own domestic bottles, which it empties for its friends, in a spirit of some rivalry. The collection of these bottles becomes a source of wealth of the most secret of cellars, a kind of precious heirloom to be left to one's descendants along with one's parchment *Consule Mario* hanging around one's neck. I drank the last of the flasks that a gentlewoman had inherited from one of her

ancestors who had been a great lover of the cask. The bottle was, of course, at least as old as its latest owner, who was well over eighty, and yet it had conserved all its sweetness. In my view sweetness is a bad feature, a veritable vice afflicting our wines; and yet I do enjoy the obliging seriousness of Montepulciano, even the austerity of Chianti. Count Francesco Algarotti wrote to His Excellency the Lord Prosecutor Zen to urge him to promote the trade of Venetian wines with the Orient. To this proposal, some people hurriedly retort that wine cannot travel. Be that as it may, I can cite two examples of evidence against this, regarding two barrels that were sent all the way to Pera and were drunk with a great deal of satisfaction. Were it true, after all, it would be a disadvantage confined to our own wines, given that navigation is normally good for others, fortifying and ennobling them. If one can drink Carmignano and Artemino in St Petersburg, why not our Grassaro or Dalla Gatta (as it is called here) in Constantinople? The temperament of our wines is not so very different from that of Greek wines. I remember once in Bologna that I served some wine from this villa of Angarano, whence I am presently writing, to thirteen people and that they all judged it to be from overseas. The fourteenth person, who considered himself a scientist of the palate, having taken several slow and serious mouthfuls to taste, declared that he was unable to decide whether it was from Samos, Tenedo or from Cyprus, but that it was without any doubt a Greek wine. At that point I judged it was time to let loose the truth and I told them that it was a wine made on my own land.[27]

Then, as now, there was always somebody ready to set themselves up as an infallible expert. Then, as now, the problem of penetrating and exporting to distant markets demanded urgent attention. After the downfall of the abhorred puritan Cromwell, the Grand Duke of Tuscany saw his chance to open up a new market for his wines in Charles II's England. Count Magalotti, an eminent expert on all things English, promptly drafted for the Grand Duke a detailed series of *Riflessioni sulla navigazione dei nostri vini per l'Inghilterra*. Flasks and barrels of Tuscany, that 'mistress of the art of manufacturing fine wines',[28] through whose wine-shops, taverns and crowded bar-rooms flowed the variety and wealth of its vineyards:

THE BOTANY OF THE PALATE   91

> Bring me here, Menghino, a smallish keg
> Of Faraone and another of Lamporecchio,
> And also bring a well of Cassero
> For the latter is brother to the other two;
> Do not bring Chianti, it grasps me by the throat
> But bring instead a bucket of Palaia
> And may Nice always keep within its arm's reach
> A huge flask of Groppoli and of Vinacciano.
>
> O what a fine thing! But I would like a sip
> Of Rochebrune, and another of Acciaio
> If you've any in your cellar: run down there now,
> My courteous host.[29]

In spite of all the exotic novelties both from the East and from the New World, traditional fruit still enjoyed pride of place on even the most opulent and sophisticated of tables. Pears were triumphant, deemed 'the only fruit that provides a truly satisfying decoration on a *dessert* and is best at satisfying our senses of taste, sight and smell, through its different species or varieties'.[30] Regarded as the gentle flame of the dinner-table, the pear displayed its warm and juicy characteristics by gracing pictorial compositions, still lifes, canvases by 'flower painters', vegetable panoplies and the overflowing baskets produced by Bartolomeo Bimbi and 'fruit painters'. For centuries pears remained the brilliant jewel of the buffet. At the threshold of the nineteenth century, at the time of Filippo Re, the pear could still boast 'more varieties than any tree',[31] and pears were 'infinitely more numerous and more sought after' than any other fruit. The jewel of Pomona, the goddess of fruit-trees, 'this tree is useful all year round to the farmer by satisfying all tastes, either with sweet pears or with sharp, or with both sweet and sharp combined, either cooked or raw – whatever way they are served they are always good'.[32] Neglected by the hedonism of newfangled Italians who prefer more costly and less meditative fruits, this little treasure trove of damp and gentle voluptuousness seems doomed to headlong decline.

Although it may seem hard to take such a high figure seriously, 'French gardeners writing at the end of the seventeenth century mention more than seven hundred sorts of edible pears'.[33] However, the *Jardinier français* by René Dahavron (Dahuron), the Duke of Brunswick's superintendent of orchards, and in particular the afterword by Monseigneur de la Quintinyé, general superintendent of gardens to His Very Christian Majesty, a work that was translated into Italian and printed by Albrizzi in Venice in 1704, 'only' records seventy-two varieties.[34] According to Cupani's estimate, confirmed by Nicosia, Prince Giuseppe del Bosco's orchards at Misilmeri in Sicily contained seventy-eight varieties. This pales, however, in comparison with the Tuscan pear cornucopia at the turn of the eighteenth century, as described by Pietro Antonio Micheli in his *Lista di tutte le frutte, che giorno per giorno dentro all'Anno sono poste alla mensa dell'Ar. e del Ser. mo Gran Duca di Toscana* (List of all the fruits which day by day throughout the year are placed on the table of His Most Serene Grand Duke of Tuscany):[35] a total of two hundred and thirty, all listed by name. Medici Tuscany easily outstripped France under the Sun King, as Iacopo Niccolò Guiducci contentedly emphasized in a letter to Cosimo III: 'I find that as regards pears Your Royal Highness is incomparably better off both for the number of good species and for their quality.'[36] So our cosmopolitan cook was lying, though in good faith, probably blinded by the dazzling Napoleonic meteor. In any case, as a mere cook, he may have been ignorant of the precise details regarding pears.

In an 'admirable race to extract new balsamic, medical and aromatic substances', the famous 'Medicean foundry' had sought to distil 'new smells' through the 'union of chemistry and botany'. This was part of a constant and subtle search for 'the most sublime perfection of smell'.[37] But with the agronomic experiments of the last Medicis, Italy and Europe as a whole (especially Holland) witnessed the birth of a rich panorama of 'new flowers, seeds, grafts and vegetables'.[38]

> Thus, even today, we can see that the Dutch have founded a branch of commerce that is based on the art of Flora, by creating hundreds of very beautiful and previously quite unknown flowers. The French say that in the last hundred and fifty years they have

bought very many new plants from them and that the herbs and vegetables are varied and coloured, no less beautiful than the flowers, and that everything has reached such a degree of perfection that, instead of the single species of chicory and the two poor species of lettuce that were then known, one can now number more than fifty of each species, all of which are excellent and fine to taste. The same is true as regards peaches, apricots and pears, for everyone knows how, if abandoned to themselves, fruit become wild and can renew and ennoble themselves with a thousand new beauties and flavours once an attempt is made to graft them artificially and to cultivate them. And equally, thanks to previously untried cross-breeding, by combining races, animals too can be improved, as we continually see with horses and sometimes with other species. Indeed, I have seen, though only among private people acting for their own pleasure, new kinds of dove and new chickens at once very fine and very useful, able to multiply in great number, which everyone could easily obtain by procuring in the same way some fine Padua cockerels and fine hens and some fine pigeons from other regions and by cleverly mixing them with our own.[39]

The 'risorgimento' or rebirth of Italy, after the country had been dragged down into the universal decadence of 'uncouth and barbarous Europe', resumed its path of renewal, 'rendering nature fertile for our needs'.

Nature is waiting for nothing other than our efforts to draw from it its inexhaustible riches by cultivating its thousand secret deposits both animal and vegetable, given that in only a short time we have obtained great advantages unknown both to our forefathers and to the ancients.[40]

New peas, new pulses and cabbages, new chickens and new doves, 'at once very fine and very useful', enhanced the eighteenth-century table, making it more varied.

By the second half of the eighteenth century, by which time the 'century of iron' seemed long since past, there were those who hoped that modern 'comforts' and 'true happiness'[41] could somehow restore the 'century of gold'.[42] And yet to the countless ancient illnesses were now added new diseases, 'new congestions and rheumatisms', 'new scurvies', 'new colics' and, above all, 'new convulsive maladies of the nerves, hypochondrias and vapours without name'.[43] The renewal of life and society that was occurring, along with new discoveries and unheard-of inventions in technology and labour, was guided by a rediscovered ability to intervene scientifically in a nature that had by this time escaped from the magical and cabalistic atmosphere of pre-Galilean culture. Not only had everyday customs and the physical landscape been overhauled, the very well-being and quality of 'public happiness' had been enhanced. Many Italian regions now offered a very different and spring-like picture, reinvigorated as they were by a wind of renewal that was both hard-working and feverish, and made itself felt in every aspect of civil life.

> The countryside has all been brought under the plough, the rivers flow at the bottom of their beds, the forests are well hewn, the castles have been demolished, houses are more spacious and comfortable, roads are maintained, food is adorned with seasonings, dishes are tasty and wines plentiful and select; people keep their bodies and skin cleaner, encouraged by the most varied supply of linen and by more convenient clothing; baths are taken more frequently and peace, calm and good taste reign everywhere; and the new enlighteners who have come into the arts, the sciences, even the manufactures and, above all, into the obligations of society and of religion seem to have brought genuine happiness along with bodily health and the virtues of the human spirit.[44]

From the sixteenth and 'golden'[45] century onwards 'thick and profound night / Begins to melt away'[46] and

> The fine achievement of ingenious fashion
> That injects new life into European trade
> And the sculpted marbles and vibrant fabrics
> Are rivalled by the works of talented minds
> Who, both daring and wise, penetrate the sombre
> Physical labyrinths.[47]

'Taste', 'grace' and the rediscovery of 'true natural beauty',[48] of 'delicate and lively feeling' and of 'harmony' had overcome 'prejudice' and 'recalcitrant ignorance'.[49] The sense of sight had rediscovered harmonic symmetry and the grace of the 'beautiful form' that 'entices the eye and fills the soul'.[50] In particular,

> When, to enjoy the placid summer's air
> In your cultivated and sweet-scented gardens
> Oh beautiful Euphrosine, you descend
> And walk slowly along those charming paths,
> When your flattering eye then alights
> On the English, Bavarian or French parterre,
> Do you not feel your senses then swell
> With the certain and regular law and the measure
> That separates, divides and imparts order to everything
> While your soul is filled with a secret pleasure?[51]

It was an intense but wholly intellectual pleasure that 'measure' and mathematized space instilled in the human senses, feeding with 'secret pleasure' souls already drunk on the sublime geometry of the garden. This extreme neoclassical stylization had embalmed the 'graceful disorder'[52] of the eighteenth-century garden in forms that a worn-out 'gracefulness' had rendered as cold and unchanging as marble. Those 1770s gardens had been inspired by the art of the 'voluptuous gardener of Aristippus',[53] by winding paths, shifting perspectives, unpredictable scenes in which the spirit might be born anew from the unexpected variations of the landscape: 'now they summon up the sweetest smells of the rarest flowers and plants; now an unimagined prospect of ancient architecture laid waste by time; here a little temple, there a park full of wild beasts, there a little navigable canal'.[54]

TEN

PERFIDIOUS ART

The Jesuit Saverio Bettinelli could not be taken in by appearances: the reflowering, indeed the 'risorgimento', was real and palpable. Every class and even the most marginalized of social groups, like beggars and convicts, now lived in more humane conditions. As the author of 'Lettere a Lesbia Cidonia' pointed out, underlinen was now changed more frequently, more baths were taken, meals were more plentiful. Everybody was a little better off. Everybody, except those who worked on the land. 'Peasants,' as G. B. Roberti remarked, 'are perhaps the only ones who, whether healthy or infirm, in my eyes appear to be neglected, though they constitute a huge number.'[1] Roberti, who was far more sensitive to humanitarian issues than was his colleague Bettinelli, noticed on his strolls through the countryside around Bologna that peasants 'are commonly wretched and would deserve to be regarded with gentler eyes by such a humane century'.

> At less than a mile from here [Bologna], on an immense plain of fertile fields, one can see the haggard and coarse faces of the peasants who live in those straw and mud slums that crack and crumble on all sides; peasants who hide their nakedness as best they can with a filthy smock cut out of rough canvas; who chew black bread, though they harvest white wheat; who drink water, though it is they who put the raw wine of their masters in its barrels. A few years ago a Royal Pontiff, in his capacity as both Pope and Sover-

eign, was obliged to issue two successive decrees in order to curtail the avidity of inexorable, arrogant and menacing tenant farmers who kept chasing from the fields already shorn of their fertile crops the ragged swarms of poor beggars who wandered around the countryside, their eyes burning with desire and their arms bowed, searching for a few ears of corn missed or forgotten by a weary or sated scythe. Weighed down with the worries of the Christian republic, Pope Benedict XIV, according to his custom, retreated far from the noise and the smoke of Rome, to the heart of a villa surrounded by green countryside, in search of some rest from public affairs; on his way bands of skinny and exhausted old men, cringing children and plaintive little girls swarmed around him and, dropping to their knees, their hands raised high, blocked the onward march of the soldiers of the papal guard. With their beseeching voices and weeping complaints, the miserable starvelings drowned out the noise of the hurrying coaches. The result was that while the carts, screeching beneath the weight of the corn piled high, reached the stores of the rich landowners, these poor wretches were prohibited, on pain of kicking and insults, from even crossing the already cropped plains in search of the slightest ear of corn that the rough thatch might hide. Of such stray ears might a thin sheaf have been formed to comfort present and future hunger. The pain and howling of these desolate peasants contaminated the sweetness of the air and, I would say, the pleasantness of that ground.[2]

Unlike Bettinelli, a cosmopolitan Jesuit who was at his ease in every salon, Roberti was very sceptical about the 'external culture' and about the 'humanity' of dazzling 'progress'.

> We are well housed, well clothed, well fed . . . but I do not know whether, for all that, we have reason to celebrate ourselves as human beings, just because we grease our hair with an ointment, because we powder it with white flour, because we have cloths cut with scissors so that they suit our shoulders, or because we place on the table big dishes and little dishes in such a way that the little dishes yield the more noble place to the dignity of the big dishes. Some debate should be necessary before we pronounce that a humanity that clothes itself according to a fashion obtaining abroad, eats in the fashion of abroad, dwells in the fashion of abroad and

combs its hair in the fashion of abroad is really to be called humanity, or not, more accurately, servitude.[3]

Faithful to Italian tradition and ways of life, Abbot Roberti was unable to appreciate fully 'the comforts and splendours' of French civilization that were being imported into Italy. 'Nowadays one exalts the ingenuity of their cuisine and the magnificence of their table. It has been said that the French alone know how to eat. Yet not long ago Monsieur Mercier wrote that the people of Paris are the worst-fed people anywhere in Europe.'[4]

Father Roberti was certainly no ascetic. He loved ham, salami, mortadella, coffee and chocolate, fine wine and tasty strawberries, sweetly scented desserts and vanilla creams. But he could bear neither French arrogance nor the fanciful and frivolous French fashions that many Italian aristocrats were hurrying with reverence to adopt. Nor could he approve of what Count Joseph de Maistre later, in the grim years of the Restoration, considered not only harmful but perverse: the criminal association between culinary experimentation and the licence that was afforded to bad writing. As he remarked to the interlocutor of one of his 'entretiens', after heaping praise on Christian fasting and exalting generalized abstinence:

> Having considered excess in quantity, now turn your mind to abuses in quality: examine in all its details this perfidious art of exciting a lying appetite that is murdering us; just think of the countless caprices of intemperance, of these seductive *compositions* which, to our bodies, are what evil books are to our mind, which is at one and the same time overloaded and corrupted by them.[5]

Abbot Roberti would never have regarded good cookery as a perfidious art or roundly cursed the 'seductive *compositions*' of skilled cooks. He simply detested the dehumanization of the century and the brilliant, so-called enlightened culture. He deplored the narrow-minded mood of indifference exhibited towards the lower classes and the erosion of any spirit of solidarity or Christian charity, especially among rich people and high-born and over-fed intellectuals. He loathed the cynicism and insensitivity of certain famous *maîtres à penser*, whom he considered monsters of blind and evil selfishness. The extraordinary anecdote that Roberti recounted about the inhumanity of Bernard Le Bovier de Fontenelle, one of the most highly lauded intellectual idols of his century, if true (the source appears to be Linguet's *Annali politici*), marks a high point of moral indifference occasioned by the pleasures of the table, the perverse achievement of a culture that could find pleasure only in its own sparkling wit.

> Abbot Dubos, Canon of Beauvais, was on familiar terms with Fontenelle, and they called one another friends. One day the Canon was dining alone with the author of the worlds when they were presented with a clump of asparagus. One wanted to season it with oil, the other with a vinaigrette. The two Socratics (wisdom, after all, does not rule out greed) agreed to divide the asparagus equally according to the taste of each man. Before the two dishes had been prepared, Abbot Dubos was struck with apoplexy. All the domestics were deeply moved. Fontenelle, the creator of fine notions, displayed great zeal and ran to the top of the stairs to cry out to the cook: 'All the asparagus in vinaigrette, all the asparagus in vinaigrette!' Once the corpse had disappeared, Fontenelle sat down to table and ate all the asparagus, providing factual proof that even apoplexy is good for something.[6]

As far as cookery was concerned, the real revolution did not occur in 1789. On the contrary, the immortal French Revolution, by decapitating the summit of the culinary pyramid, that is to say the King, laid the foundations for a democratic and representative cuisine and ushered into existence the bourgeois cook, the family cook and the domestic cook. It also marked a shift towards a form of commercial, venal and mass catering that was quite prepared – in return for payment – to popularize and vulgarize the secrets of the great aristocratic cuisines. Influenced by Condillac, the real gastronomic revolution was reformist and sensualist and occurred under the shadow of the *style rocaille*. Its theoreticians were Enlightenment reformers who, along with the devotees of age-old Gothic, scholastic and baroque cookery, sought to enclose the magnificent and indigestible grammar of bloated and fussy baroque cuisine in a 'temple of ignorance'. The intellectual agility and nimbleness of up-and-coming generations called for a corresponding lightness of touch in culinary procedures. Eating to excess in an atmosphere of pomp and ceremony, while sunk in huge old armchairs, rather than perched on the latest skimpy and uncomfortable Louis XV chairs, was no longer the done thing. Fashionable society turned its nose up at food heaped high and preferred to eat with a studied lack of appetite and a display of ill-concealed impatience towards the old feudal and patriarchal type of cuisine. The same shift in taste could be seen at work in the world of fashion among those women who frequented the salons in 'andriennes' (long-skirted dressing-gowns), painted with 'frivolous little images of small animals and wispy plants'. The new rage was for 'frivolous design', 'Chinese mixtures', 'elegant and fragile frippery', 'curious *galanteries*', 'frivolous fragility', 'flippant whimsy' and ubiquitous variety. For all such 'elegant butterflies'[7] the kitchen too had to produce pretty little trifles. For a dyspeptic and nocturnal society, for women who woke late ('in bed at midday, she awaited her chocolate / Seated in a pretty posture')[8] but who were none the less at the very heart of social communication, for a high society that lived 'in conversations and in a perpetual round of visits and tittle-tattle', for a 'noble caste' that 'had to struggle to get through each long day', the table became one more venue at which to talk, another chance for prolonged conversations. Food was spoken rather than eaten, taken with detachment, while the new hot beverages (coffee, tea, chocolate) punctuated the passage of time with an obligatory ritual and etiquette. 'Certain drinks', Abbot Roberti pointed out, 'are a form of welcome that, according to normal ritual, are not appreciated if offered but may offend if forgotten.'[9]

Night replaced day.

> Staying up very late is typical of gentlemen . . . The light of the sun is ignoble . . . one tells stories, gambles and dines by the light of wax candles, whereas one lives in prison beneath precisely cut panes of glass, in air that is ventilated yet remains hard to breathe.

For how long a time have how many people not seen the dawn! Or if they do see it, it is on their way home from the theatre, sleepy and shut in, and they certainly do not wish to see it. Certain ladies never sleep at night . . . which is why in Paris such ladies are prettily called *lampes*.[10]

For these ladies and their companions it became increasingly difficult to eat with appetite.

> Our delicate ladies, tottering with nausea, cast a listless eye over the food and agree, when begged, to taste this and that. Having lazed around in bed all day, following the interminable idleness of preparation, their muscles go weak, their humours no longer cleanse themselves and their digestion does not function properly. This is why their appetite, which is the best seasoning food can have, is blunt and languishes.[11]

And indeed it must have demanded an increasing amount of effort to arouse their appetite with 'tempting titbits', to find food sufficiently titillating to excite their 'idle juices' from their torpor. For such sensitive devotees of the cult of Divine Sloth, light and caressing diets were necessary, velvety dishes that just slipped down, sweet and soft, standing with whimsical gracefulness on delicate little tables, with finely turned legs. In some houses tables had become frighteningly bare. A little worried by this, G. B. Roberti commented:

> Several fashionable tables are really very limited. I have on occasion dined with golden cutlery when there was nothing to eat . . . ; those who live an inert life out of step with the world around them ordinarily eat very little; and more than one such gentleman, on account of the disturbance of his health, is obliged to make do at lunch with a boiled chicken and a vegetable soup, just to ward off scurvy.[12]

Unlike women of the previous century who had loved to feed greedily on strong-tasting foods, these languid, dyspeptic, salon-frequenting women, lacking in appetite and conversing so coldly that they ran the risk of passing out, were fearful of the heated, animal tastes of instinctual luxury and flesh. Love too, like food, was more spoken and observed than enjoyed. In line with social procedures, the widespread practice of libertinism signified an intellectualization of erotic play and a lazy and listless use of the body.

Hot-blooded baroque femininity had displayed womanly characteristics of a quite different character. Catherine of Braganza, wife of Charles II of England, enjoys an important place in the gallery of hot-blooded seventeenth-century women. Reporting back to his extremely bigoted master, Cosimo III, Lorenzo Magalotti, that most refined 'Florentine spy', poked his indiscreet nose into Catherine's private life and pored over her most secret physiological behaviour and sexual preferences. The Portuguese noblewoman, who was of an 'extraordinarily heated and inflamed temperament . . . with a great effervescence of the blood' and 'often subject to extraordinary purges . . . [is] by her very nature immeasurably sensitive to pleasures'. Indeed 'sweet pleasure attains such a high point in her that, after the ordinary outpouring of humours that from women too may be squeezed by the violence of taste, such a great quantity of blood flows from her genital parts that sometimes it does not cease for several days'.[13]

It seemed to Magalotti that such an excess of hot liquids, viscous humours and shattering pleasures was most likely caused by the 'immoderate use of powdered spices in food, and of amber and musk in confectionery'. Excesses of this kind tended to become rarer during the eighteenth century, which in its smells, flavours and scents rapidly distanced itself from the recent past.

> The delicious ladies of the fifteenth and sixteenth centuries, and even those of the last century, in particular the Spanish . . . were always strongly scented. Musk, amber and incense did not offend them; nowadays, ladies faint and are shaken by convulsions on impact even with the spirit of balm. If you ask those learned physicians the reason, which I do not know, for such a strange difference in affections, some might suggest that their temperaments have been woven in a different form than in the past. Sometimes I am indeed touched by the suspicion that in all such

disdain for odours there must be at least some degree of simpering and mannered affectation.[14]

The horror that intellectual and gallant ladies of the eighteenth century felt towards amber, their aversion for musk in confectionery and their revulsion at highly spiced and strong-smelling dishes help to provide a more accurate and detailed portrait of women who were endowed with a penchant not only for wearisome conversation and nocturnal party games but also for a sophisticated and elegant eroticism that seemed to flit to and fro above a delicate net of rituals of distancing and estrangement rather than of sensual abandonment. It therefore seems reasonable to suppose that a diet that was enlightened by reason and disencumbered of the most oppressive of the baser senses was not particularly conducive to carnal passions of an intensity comparable to those that coursed through the veins of such women as Catherine of Braganza. Eighteenth-century ladies, who, according to Abbot Galiani, loved more with their head than with their heart, were women who find that 'even roses stink', as Pietro Chiari, a priest and novelist from Brescia, memorably wrote.[15] The dining-table had to be immaculately presented, shrouded by a play of appearances and pretence, and dishes had to be disguised as in an interminable comedy of errors. As Abbot Chiari wrote in a letter in 1749 to a 'lady of quality':

> The great evil of this era is that as far as vegetables, fruits, fish, animals and fowl are concerned, nature no longer knows what to produce to suit our tastes and our wishes. Foods used in the past are no longer worthy of us unless, on arrival in our kitchens, they abandon both their form and their name. To transform them, we bring into play all the tree barks and all the drugs that America has delivered into our hands since we discovered her. A thousand ingredients are required for each dish, which, in the end, tastes of none of them; and even those who lick their chops and slaver over such food cannot say at all what it is. Without knowing what it is engaged upon, human gluttony strives to draw from fruit, roots and vegetables ever newer condiments for ancient dishes. To this purpose, they keep victuals simmering away on the stove for hour

upon hour, thus diminishing their most life-giving juices and substantial vigour. Cooks are more prized today than were sculptors in Athens; and yet, if one weighs everything fairly, they ought to be held equal to the crudest of potters. Potters, thanks to the wheel and to firing, are able to make the clay assume the shape of a jug or of a bottle, while remaining just clay. Cooks, on the other hand, disguise meat, which remains just meat, in a thousand different ways. Poor people! They are to be forgiven in so many regards, for if they did not proceed in this way, they would find no patrons and would therefore starve to death. At every quite ordinary table, there must be at least one hundred dishes of an appearance and taste that are not only very different but opposed among themselves, never before tried and all excessively extravagant. Any kind of food used by ordinary people is straight away ruled out: fruits and vegetables in season and fish of middling size; all such articles could appear on this table only if skilfully disguised, so that the devil himself would not recognize them for what they really are... Next, what is needed is the strange and extremely rare – strawberries in January, grapes in April, artichokes in September. If only, Madame, these choices, these transformations and these precautions were able to satisfy human gluttony; if the delicacy of modern palates did not turn our stomachs the whole day through. At the slightest whiff of onion or of garlic many women roll their eyes or fall into a faint; and all the balms and quintessences used in two Egyptian funerals do not suffice to bring them round. Countess X finds that quail make her stomach heavy; pastries thicken the blood; milk exalts the bile; lettuces purge the stomach; drugs inflame the throat; oysters spoil the appetite; and two small drops of wine from our own region give her the most terrible head vapours. And at your own very sumptuous table, I have on several occasions observed the wife of lawyer X, who, as hungry as the she-wolf that nursed Romulus and Remus, could not find a single main course that was quite to her liking. Performing on her plate a precise anatomy of every dish that is presented to her, she turns the food over and over with her fork, lifts it up and flips it over, examines it from above, from below, at its sides, from within and from without, as if she were not quite sure from which end she should begin to eat it. She wrinkles her nose, half closes her eyes, twists her mouth up when she tastes it; if this bit is too bland, then that bit must be too salty; if this is too sweet, that is too sour; sometimes it is too hot, sometimes too cold; either it is hard, or it is falling all to pieces; she likes her food neither fatty nor too lean; with neither lemon nor sugar; seasoned with neither oil nor vinegar; accompanied by neither bread nor biscuit; washed down with neither water nor wine; she favours neither roast meat nor boiled; yet, with all her devouring grimaces and her famished airs, there is nothing that afflicts her, neither ailment nor care.[16]

The simpering, contrived anorexia of the bewigged ladies of the enlightened eighteenth century appears all the more striking when contrasted with the bulimia of the sweet-scented ladies of the seventeenth century. The listlessness, faddishness, languid indifference to food, calculated lack of appetite, ornate affectation and ostentatious craving for physical lightness and intellectual agility became such widely fashionable mannerisms that even the ladies' table companions were infected: in a letter entitled 'De' cibi appruovati, e disappruovati dall'uso' (Of foods approved and disapproved for use) Abbot Chiari remarked that

> Baron X performs every action with the very same delicacy that characterized Narcissus... the more dishes he orders, the fewer mouthfuls he eats... As a worshipper of peculiarity and of affectation in gestures, he is quite capable of eating bread with his fork and tart with his spoon... To discover the most delicate part of a chicken, he can create a cemetery of gnawed bones; and he will dip his spoon angrily into the bottom of a pot of sauce, in an attempt to fish out a mushroom. If by chance he is seated next to a lady, through his encouragements to her to eat he will make her lose all appetite; not content to cut everything on her plate into mouth-sized morsels, he wants to use his delicate fingers as a fork with which to serve her and entreats the lady to let herself be force-fed like a goose.[17]

In a world such as this, where the dream of lightness could be transformed into a social imperative and a dominant preoccupation, the 'plurality of loves' and the inconstancy of feelings could generate a broad array of pleasures. Of these, the supreme pleasure of sight pushed the attraction exerted by table pleasures into the background. If, next to the *Tempio del gusto*, one opens the *Tempio dell'infedeltà* ('betrayal seems a virtue', as Carlo Innocenzo Frugoni sang), the new devotees of these worldly rites, presented with appetizing and inviting dishes, appeared to caress them with their eyes rather than to taste them against their palate.

Dishes had to present a picture that was pleasing to the eye, a sort of delicate and varied landscape, as pretty and voluptuous as an Arcadian pastoral, village fête or garden entertainment for young lovers. It became essential 'to paint and represent the dishes'[18] and to pander to the eye with 'lots of sauces, colours and shapes' as well as a variety of 'strange and lying' names.[19] The aim was to provide a meal that was as light and chirpy as a song set to music, as flirtatious as a love poem, as pretty as a *petite poésie*, as highly polished and intricate as any cameo. A foretaste of the pleasures of the imagination was provided by the refinement of the meal itself, whose role, rather than to satisfy and satiate, was to prepare and predispose the diners for *rêverie*, for a sentimental journey, for embarkation to Cythera. Those with particoloured minds, *the bigarrures de l'espirit*, loved to be delicately alluded to in polychrome pastels, in variegated and dappled tasty titbits, sugar-coated *petits riens*, elegant sugary little morsels, while their ears were caressed by whispered *chansonnettes*.

In the eighteenth century good taste meant seeing and catching the scent of something rather than chewing and swallowing it. The separation of sight and taste became accentuated and sight developed into a shrewd and cautious antenna in the service of taste. There was a preference for looking at flowers rather than smelling their scent, and people sought to embalm spring in exquisite artificial gardens made of porcelain, silk, canvas, wax, paper, feathers or, when it came to the dining-table, in 'sugar and sweets'.

> One winter's day Madame de Pompadour invited to her famous house *Bellevue* none other than Louis XV, whose mind she always sought to rouse from the boredom of uniformity by means of novel spectacles. The King was seated in an extraordinarily decorated room when, through the magic operation of secret machines, the moving chamber turned in silence and was transported over a most

refined garden, perfectly reproduced, painted with porcelains which, as it were, strewed it with flowers.[20]

Roberti, in a letter to a 'most elegant and noble lady' who had sent him a chamber garden made of silk and canvas, admitted to her that,

> without having to make the journey, and comfortably installed in the depths of my armchair, I contemplate at my great leisure in this winter of 1784 a garden in my office . . . It is true that these French flowers were made of porcelain: but that means that their life had a few extra degrees of uncertainty, since they could break more easily. I therefore prize the light canvas and silk flowers that you, most generous lady, have so graciously donated to me, more highly than those of any other kind.[21]

In its 'delectation for odours' the eighteenth century broke with the 'grand voluptuous metaphysics'[22] of the baroque age, inspired by the 'Spanish metaphysics' of 'pastes and powders'. Once the new fashions had been transplanted into Italy, they attained such heights of sophistication and such ecstasies of voluptuousness among the 'mystical gluttons' that the 'members of the Accademia degli Odoristi of Tuscany . . . felt contempt for any fragrance that was not at once outlandish, multi-layered and exquisite; and if they stooped to smell a mere rose, it was only by way of mortification'.[23]

ELEVEN

INDIAN BROTH

The eighteenth century's gradual break with the taste and fashion of the preceding century may be captured in the shift away from the complicated taste of baroque chocolate, thick with pungent aromas, towards the simpler and less composite taste of Enlightenment chocolate, which was prepared by simply blending sugar and cocoa with a light dusting of vanilla and cinnamon.

In the second half of the seventeenth century Francesco Redi noted that its

> use in Europe has become extremely common, especially at the courts of princes and in noble houses, since it is believed to fortify the stomach and to have a thousand other effects beneficial to health. The Spanish court was the first in Europe to begin using chocolate. Indeed, the Spanish know how to handle chocolate to a point of perfection: yet our era and the court of Tuscany have found a way of enhancing Spanish perfection with a dash of even more exquisite nobility, thanks to new European ingredients and a newly discovered way of adding fresh rinds of citrons and lemons; and the sweet smell of jasmine, mixed with cinnamon, vanilla, amber and musk, makes the chocolate smell quite wonderful to whoever is enjoying it.[1]

Such 'exquisite nobility' had, however, to remain interred in the palaces of the Medicis. As in the case of the 'jasmine of the heart', Cosimo considered the formula a state secret that had to be jealously guarded from falling into foreign hands. The order that he gave to his chief physician and spicery superintendent was unambiguous: the procedures and quantities required for the preparation of jasmine-flavoured chocolate should in no case leave the Grand Duchy's 'foundry'. In 1680 Diacinto Cestoni, a skilled apothecary and microscopist from Leghorn with a tireless specialist interest in chameleons, asked Francesco Redi for the recipe. Although Redi was a man of a generally kind disposition and particularly attached to Cestoni – a member, after all, of Redi's own team of researchers – the letter that he wrote in reply displays the disappointment he felt at receiving such an unwelcome request.

> I am very sorry that you should ask me about such a matter, which I have been expressly ordered not to disclose. That is to say, how one prepares jasmine-scented chocolate. What I am able to tell you is that it does not involve jasmine water since, when one kneads cocoa, it does not mix with water and although one can manage to introduce into it a few drops of jasmine water, it is not enough to impart its scent to the whole mass of chocolate. And if one added a lot of this water, the chocolate would not hold together well. I know that you are discreet and that you are well aware of the limits within which you may speak of this.[2]

Redi's reticence is not so hard to understand if one recalls not only that he was chief physician at Casa Medici and in charge of the Grand Duchy's spicery but that as a devoted confidant and courtier he could on no account divulge secrets that served to cheer up an otherwise hypochondriac and taciturn prince. After Cosimo's death the recipe finally leaked out and, by way of Cestoni, 'chocolate with the smell of jasmines' reached the great naturalist Antonio Vallisnieri.

> Take 10 pounds of black cocoa, clean it and crush it into bits. Take a sufficient quantity of fresh jasmine and mix it with the cocoa, laying it out in successive layers in a box or other container, and leave it there for 24 hours. Then remove it and add an equal quantity of cocoa, spreading it out layer after layer as above, and once every 24 hours add fresh jasmine, in all 10 or 12 times. Then

take 8 pounds of perfectly dry good white sugar; 3 ounces of perfect vanilla; 6 ounces of perfect cinnamon; and 2 scruples of ambergris. Then proceed to make the chocolate according to best practice. Take care to ensure that the stone is not too hot and that the artisan kneads the chocolate properly. Its mass should not exceed 4 or 5 pounds. If the stone is overheated, the chocolate will lose its fragrance.[3]

This mysterious recipe, which greedy apothecaries and wild enthusiasts for 'Indian broth' dreamed about and yearned for and which was kept secret in the safe of the foundry at Palazzo Pitti, would no longer arouse anyone's interest. The century of odour-fanatics and of Cyrano de Bergerac was a period when noses were indeed big. They were regarded as intellectual channels that led directly to the precious seat of intelligence, in close touch with damp cerebral matter itself. Noses suddenly fitted into the mock-heroic epic, became an object of meditations on physiognomy, crept into burlesque poems of the type written by Francesco Berni, cropped up in sermons, inspired entire treatises on plastic surgery and raised laughs in the grotesquely distorting ballads of popular poetry. In Florence a preacher once gave 'a sermon on noses in the presence of the Grand Duchess' and detailed 'so many sorts and such ridiculous noses that I cannot believe that there can ever have been so many, even in the land of the *Nasamoni*, who are known to feed on smells'.[4] In the second half of the century the scent and flavour of chocolate exercised an irresistible attraction on the noses and palates of princes and cardinals, doctors and Jesuits. Francesco Redi, already an eminent apothecary, turned into an ingenious forwarding agent, supervising the odorous strategy and amber-scented diplomacy conceived by Cosimo, a fanatical collector of jasmine and of jasmine-flavoured chocolate. In 1689 a precious package was dispatched from the Florentine palace, addressed to Father Paolo Antonio Appiani of the Society of Jesus. It contained the 'chocolate that, in your note, you say you desire. It is contained in six packets of six different sorts, of which the amber-scented, the Spanish and the jasmine-flavoured sorts should be the best.'[5] The previous year Redi had sent a case full of rare and unheard-of delicacies to another Jesuit, Father Tommaso Strozzi, accompanying the gift with a very strongly scented letter.

> Just try a little of this powder of Tonc. I think that Your Reverence has certainly never tasted it, for it is the new fashion, a fashion that only people of high rank share among themselves; it is pure powder, as produced by Mother Nature, without any artifice at all in its scent. I am sending you only a small amount, for only a very few chosen people are entitled to it. I am also sending other powders in greater quantity, hyacinth, vanilla, daffodil, lily of the valley, amber, Greek musk and another pure musk from Brazil. As for the jasmine-scented chocolate, I have sent you twelve packets so that you can take it to Naples to taste with your friends.[6]

Lorenzo Magalotti, who was not only the secret adviser and grey eminence of the Medici spicery but also the tutelary deity of confectionery, liqueurs, perfumes, cream pastes and powders, had brought back from Spain a full notebook on aromatic confectionery. Magalotti was the secret expert of the buffet who supplied Francesco Redi with recipes for citrus-flavoured chocolate, jasmine-scented chocolate, chocolate with frangipane, pastilles and flower-scented chocolates.

Such tasty and precious samples were bound to have an effect. Having converted to the cult of the new manna, Father Strozzi immediately set about composing a 'very gallant poem'. This was partly in response to an entreaty from the Grand Duchy's chief physician through whose hands all the overseas marvels arriving on the quayside at Leghorn had to pass. The learned priest's poem took the form of a long and carefully constructed recipe in refined Latin verse in which the 'eminent theologian and distinguished preacher of the Society of Jesus', instead of imparting techniques for evading eternal damnation, taught the 'way to handle chocolate paste, how to reduce it into the form of a drink whenever one wishes to take it'.[7] Chocolate and eternal happiness were not incompatible.

The collective infatuation for 'chocolate', for which Jesuits had been the emissaries, eulogists, pioneers and importers, seems to have left other Catholic circles and religious orders almost untouched. The Dominicans, the traditional rivals of the Society of Jesus, as well as many other orders took a firm stand against the 'use, or rather the abuse, of certain aromatic plants in the beverage from Mexico known as chocolate'.[8] Several years before Father Strozzi had immersed himself in the deepest secrets of chocolate technology, Father Giuseppe Girolamo Semenzi, a regular clergyman and professor of theology at the University of Pavia, had tasted with some suspicion the 'Indian broth' and had warned against the hidden dangers of what he believed to be an insidious beverage liable to overheat the blood.

> The Indian ship carries to European lips
> The sugars of Brazil, the nuts of Banda,
> And strong-smelling goods originating from
> The Moluccas, Ceylon and other strange shores.
>
> Both Spain and Holland manufacture frothy
> Ambrosias for a vain and gluttonous thirst;
> And inhuman Asia embalms clay pots
> And wreathes them around our civilized Italy.
>
> Now vanilla, now cocoa is named,
> And, full of fragrance, this majestic luxury
> Is as good as when taken at Memphis or at Rome.
>
> Often, however, it inflames the blood parched
> By too much heat and too many aromas
> And taste turns remedy to poison.[9]

The cleric's sonnet seems to betray a hint of disapproval for the exoticizing rage that was then flooding even the most out of the way sanctuaries of 'non-barbarian Europe'. The cocoa that was used in the preparation of 'frothy ambrosias' and in hot chocolates designed to satisfy 'vain and gluttonous thirst' was regarded with the same ill-concealed contempt that was vented on the Chinese porcelain with which 'inhuman Asia' was overwhelming 'civilized Italy'.

Not all Catholic circles accepted the introduction of chocolate into social rituals with an equal warmth and enthusiasm. This was not so much on account of the Hispanic and clerical character of this Catholic and Jesuitical beverage (whatever may have been hastily written to this effect)[10] as on medical and economic grounds.[11] Coffee, on the other hand, which according to one rather clumsy historical interpretation has been identified as a beverage congenial to the Protestant ethic, a symbol of hard bourgeois graft and nordic business acumen, found converts and enthusiasts in many Catholic circles throughout southern Europe.

In another sonnet the same theologian reviewed one by one the 'remedies of health-giving plants' available in his *Mondo Creato* and added to the list 'cauè, or coffee, a beverage that is made from the fruit of a tree from Happy Arabia, whence it has been brought into Italy'.

> The crushed fruit of oriental trees simmers
> At the bottom of a copper pan, and in the silvery water
> A mixture wrought with the frothing sugar
> Makes the warm drenched scent yet sweeter still.
> The steam creates a precious cloud,
> A sweet-scented antidote to languishing heads
> Providing life-giving juice, a tasty infusion,
> A rivulet purging the breast of every illness.
> I drink Indian ambrosia in a handsome cup
> And, with coffee combined, there flows into my soul
> A curative power and a calming joy.
> Humanity may therefore itself console
> Though the world be injured in its innermost parts
> Greed at least still possesses the balms of Arabia.[12]

Regardless of the reservations of doctors or economists, chocolate (which, besides, in the authoritative view of many distinguished theologians, could be consumed without breaking the Lent fast), embarked upon a triumphal march, matched by the equally irresistible progress made by coffee. In a matter of a few decades the conquest was so well consolidated that even Bacchus, cast up on the shores of America, at last converted to the new drink:

> Having put on
> A placid face
> The fiery god
> Said merrily:
> This, my maenads,
> This, my satyrs
> This is currently called:
> A royal and life-giving drink or,
> In the American tongue, 'chocolate'.[13]

The defeat of the tottering god was spectacular: only a score or so years had passed since he had solemnly sworn that none of the new beverages would ever pass his lips:

> Never shall I be seen
> Using either chocolate or tea,
> For any such medicine
> Would never do for me:
> I would rather sip venom
> Than a glass of most loathsome,
> Bitter and dangerous coffee.

Yet not only had he become accustomed to drinking the 'celestial beverage',[14] 'the sweet white juice / of Indian cane'[15] (the same that Metastasius offered Phyllis, teaching her the recipe), he had even had to suffer the ultimate indignity of sipping 'a liquor so repulsive, / So black and so muddy' fit only for slaves and janizaries, a sombre hellish drink invented by the Furies.

In the eighteenth century Bacchus' reign underwent a miserable series of setbacks: coffee invaded Europe, hot chocolate aroused frenzies on all sides, England in the second half of the century became 'the Land of Tea' (Hugh Honour); even cider managed to find its way into Italy. After its praises were sung by Magalotti, who translated John Philips's short poem 'The Cider' into Italian,[16] cider appears to have found favour with Cosimo III, to the huge disappointment of a Tuscan Bacchus who railed furiously and uncontrollably against the 'loathsome harvest' of 'fine dew-covered apples'[17] perpetrated in the very gardens of Palazzo Pitti and under the benevolent gaze of the penultimate Grand Duke.

Bowls, cups and chocolate pots soon became part of the domestic panorama of mansions, villas, bishops' palaces, convents and other well-appointed homes:

> The champion drink
> That takes the crown
> And beats the rest,
> Is chocolate
> Which thick with foam
> Both boils and steams.[18]

New abuses came to light and unprecedented excesses were perpetrated. Certain unrestrained gluttons took to drinking vast quantities of the Mexican nectar, thereby indulging in a form of behaviour that verged on drug abuse. 'A single cup at least three hours before meals is quite enough; yet there are certain gluttons who surely harm their health by traipsing from one side of the city to the other and aping those errand boys in Rome who drink three or four cups every morning if so many are served them.'[19]

At the beginning of the eighteenth century the rituals of cocoa consumption had not yet become hard and fast and the techniques to be followed in its preparation were still a matter of confused and lurching experiment. If cocoa was not actually misused, its use was certainly surrounded by many uncertainties and errors of method. Those new to cocoa were particularly prone to eccentric ideas and the versatility of cocoa was often rashly overestimated.

> Some are so stupid
> That, with a puff,
> They blow away the froth
> At the top of the cup.

    Others propose toasts
As if drinking wine
At dinner, and thus
Empty several cups.
    Connoisseurs of cocktails
Try concocting spirits
Mixing in some chocolate
But all they make is ink.
    The dire initiative
Of mixing this drink
With blackish pasta
Is a thing I abhor,
And if that's an economy
I cannot think it's worth it.
    Nor am I persuaded
By those who perfume
Their tobacco with cocoa
And cram their nostrils withal.
    With nausea must I witness
Those gluttonous sects
Renouncing pure water
For cocoa in thick stock.
And by my faith how they rile me
Those who mix it with coffee
Or water boiled with tea.
    There are those who add egg yolk
But a greater hotchpotch
A more illusory mixture
I could never discover . . .
    Chefs too, on some strange whim,
Stuff it in their pastries
And fill a thousand little boxes
With candies made from cocoa.
But all that's achieved thereby
Is to turn a fine drink
Into the blandest of meal.
    A cook one time, finding no
Cheese in his kitchen,
Sprinkled his polenta
With chocolate that he grated

From two large squares:
So well received was this novelty
That gourmets demanded the recipe.
  Dining at a banquet
I tasted it in sauce,
But to tell the simple truth
It doesn't sharpen appetite.
  It's been already used in nougat,
It has pride of place in cakes:
One day I hope a cook
Will serve it roast with quail.[20]

Francesco Arisi dedicated this long dithyramb on the 'delicate beverage for which cups are prepared in the most majestic palaces of the most venerable princes and prelates' to Alessandro Litta, Bishop of Cremona. Among many other 'disorders',[21] Arisi counted the blameworthy custom of taking cocoa iced rather than boiling, and on these grounds reproached

  those listless people
Who in June and July
On scorching days
Guzzle chocolate,
Cold, nay freezing,
Gulping it down
In lumps of ice.[22]

As regards the alternation between cold and hot, iced and boiling, the eighteenth century was inclined towards a tolerant and sweet-tempered eclecticism. However headlong the rout of the seventeenth-century passion for icy-cold drinks and however irresistible the advance and final triumph of such hot drinks as coffee, tea and chocolate, the eighteenth century none the less saw a universal revival of affection for sorbets, ice-creams, syrups, iced waters and other beverages: almond, milk and lemon sorbet; citron, jasmine and lime water.

The baroque age was dominated by the bitter-sweet nightmare of the enema and of great and terrible purges (Molière's Argan is the best-known prototype of this kind of base and filthy slavishness). Throughout the seventeenth century there raged a momentous dispute over the social and therapeutic use of tobacco. Even James I of England entered the fray with a diatribe against the newly arrived weed, railing in his *Counter-blaste to tobacco* against 'this vile custom of tobacco taking'. Yet it was during this same period that cooling techniques were used to broaden and enrich the range of available pleasures. A 'cultural' hero such as Cardinal Moncada, with his voluptuous and well-lubricated enemas, was not an isolated case. The 'luxury' entailed in blowing hot tobacco smoke into the anus by means of a tube, however solid the *pro sanitate tuenda* arguments involved, cannot escape the suspicion that attaches to all contorted and complicated technologies that conspire to smuggle in pleasure disguised as health.

> What is more notable . . . is that nowadays, in every foreign country and even here among us, numerous men, confidently and without danger, absorb through their mouths tobacco smoke, with which, as a result, the palate and surrounding parts are impregnated, and they can then skilfully chase it out through their eyes, ears and nostrils; in this regard, luxury has made such progress that they have invented a most ingenious and very comfortable way of making such smoke pass through certain small channels buried under snow, from which it then emerges so glacial that even the coldest of north winds could not rival it. Many, not content to absorb the smoke through the mouth, relying on a new art and a new instrument, as if accomplishing a cleansing, fill their bowels with this hot smoke, and they find it beneficial for many of the most persistent illnesses, and in particular for colic pain.[23]

Ambivalence in the use of tobacco (cold if taken orally, hot if *intra nates* – introduced into the bowels through the rectum) is mirrored in the new way of drinking and in the twin-track approach to temperature that new products from overseas introduced into the lives of the wealthy. In the second half of the seventeenth century the habit of taking cold drinks had been one of the clearest signals of a liberation from an age-old medical rule prohibiting the consumption of chilled drinks by people with fevers. It was perhaps the greatest blow to the still powerful galenic edifice when 'after a heavy battle, the liver, which in its day had spilled so much blood, was at last defeated'.[24] Magalotti wittily commented that modern anatomists.

> have waged war on all the mistakes made by the ancients; and after a long series of discoveries and victories . . . , they have overthrown it [the liver], and, deeming it a gregarious viscus, and nothing less than idle, they have at last buried it alive, and have celebrated its funeral to mark its ignominy rather than to cover it with honour.[25]

The dethronement of the liver and the declaration of death of its 'empire', proclaimed in 1653 in a memorable epigram by the famous Danish anatomist Thomas Barholin, had led to a remarkable about-turn in the treatment of a number of diseases: famous doctors such as Redi now advised people to 'stuff their bellies with Morello cherries picked before the dew has lifted'. This was to be done in the morning on an empty stomach, springtime purges effected by basketfuls of strawberries, 'blow-outs with sweet figs' and 'in the throes of tertian fever' 'a cup of Morellos or of chilled plums'.[26]

Right at the start of the seventeenth century the crumbling of the ancient scientific paradigm – that is, the discovery of the central importance of the heart and the demotion of the liver to the rank of 'gregarious viscus' – went hand in hand with the gradual abandonment of the 'mistaken and extremely harmful opinion that the stomach was cold'.[27] This paved the way for a revolutionary breakthrough in the treatment of fever attacks, though it had been strictly prohibited by ancient medicine, which, confined to areas as yet untouched by modern science, still survived in Spain, a country that in comparison with Italy, France and England remained culturally very backward. In 1680, in one of his letters against atheism, Magalotti sketched a striking little picture of Spanish life in which wealthy patients gave themselves up to 'visual swigs'. In particular, he recalled that

> in Madrid, about forty years ago, there was a man who, during the summer months, had a strange but also very gallant and ingenious

way of living. He roamed around the houses of high-ranking fever sufferers during the hours when they were at their hottest; and since, at that time, enduring thirst was deemed as good a way to treat a fever as quenching it is nowadays, he let them drink with their eyes that which they could not drink with their mouth, in the following way. He would arrive at the bedside and, holding in his two hands a great glass refreshment jug all misted over and its sides streaming because of the frozen water it contained, he would then toast the health of the patient, raise the jug to his lips and, closing his eyes and displaying the same happiness with which others would swallow the contents of a smallish jar, he drank the jug dry without stopping to catch his breath. My brother, who had on more than one occasion found himself obliged to pay a doubloon each for such visual swigs, told me of the ineffability of what he had felt at that moment, a mixture of greed, comfort, amazement, sweetness and a melting sensation.[28]

Francesco Redi, who treated his own stomach condition with 'blow-outs with sweet figs', was a doctor of cautious counsel and enlightened scepticism. 'After so many centuries of doctors and poets,' he once said with a laugh, 'it is no less difficult to find a new recipe in medicine than a new thought in love'.[29] But Redi became the most convinced champion of the efficacy of ice combined with wine.

> But let it be frozen, and finished with ice,
> And see that the ice be as virginly nice,
> As the coldest that whistles from wintry skies.
> Coolers and cellarets, crystal with snows,
> Should always hold bottles in ready repose.
> Snow is good liquor's fifth element;
> No compound without it can give content;
> For weak is the brain, and I hereby scout it,
> That thinks in hot weather to drink without it.
> Bring me heaps from the shady valley:
> Bring me heaps
> Of all that sleeps
> On every village hill and alley.[30]

The Bacchus of Tuscany, who lived 'constantly / In the desire for extreme cold', had adopted a refrigeration technology that made use of natural grottoes and artificial reservoirs (the so-called conserves where snow brought from the highest Apennine ranges could be stored). The *cantimplora* also played an important role. This was an ingenious glass receptacle that, 'while it can be filled with wine, has in its middle a chamber, in which bits of ice or snow can be placed to cool the wine. It also has a long broad neck, rising from one side of the vase like a watering-can spout. At present [in Redi's day] this instrument is no longer much in use and the name *cantimplora* is now used at court to denote those pails, of silver or some other metal, that can lodge one or several glass carafes and are used for cooling wine or water by means of ice.'[31]

The decline of the glass *cantimplora* and its gradual replacement by the metal pail went hand in hand with the change undergone by styles of conviviality, which developed from the sumptuous one-dimensional Renaissance and baroque banquet to the eighteenth-century splintering of meals into a series of intimate ceremonials at which hot and cold drinks were taken in alternation according to the time of day. Hot drinks seemed to be preferred during the day, at private moments and in enclosed areas (the bedroom, the boudoir). Tea, coffee and cocoa were consumed in intimate and private circumstances, at the morning meal (*petit déjeuner*), during the *lever* or on waking up, at unofficial luncheons, at informal or confidential meetings (*petit souper*). With the exception of summer afternoon snacks, cold drinks were consumed at formal banquets and solemn receptions. Pots of chocolate, tea, coffee and sorbets divided the day between them and marked the passage of the seasons. The alternation of hot and cold drinks highlighted the shift that had taken place away from meals of the old style, dominated by chilled and iced drinks. Social spectacle oscillated within a 'fiction / partly boiling / and partly frozen', prisoner to a 'flattering' and 'lying' 'knavish court' that offered one hot fiction and one cold.[32]

TWELVE

MAD AND STARTLING NAMES

As the seventeenth century gave way to the eighteenth, in a giddying rush of days and bright-lit nights well befitting an age that undertook to reform the present by dismantling the past, the old tried and tested synergy between mouth and nose appeared slowly to crumble. A number of strange figures of the late baroque age, of the seventeenth century as it entered Arcadia, were beginning to vacate the stage. There were fewer and fewer such 'gentleman know-alls' as Giovan Battista D'Ambra, a Florentine *fin de siècle* dandy, an aesthete friend of Magalotti. The eccentric anatomist Lorenzo Bellini, who had investigated the instruments of oral pleasure in his *Gustus organum novissime deprehensum* (Newly discovered organs of taste; 1665), wrote in *Bucchereide* that Cavaliere D'Ambra had 'even a virtuoso mouth, and nose'.[1] D'Ambra was prey to an all-absorbing and exclusive obsession with smells, a mystique of aromas that aspired to a progressively enhanced understanding that was to be achieved through an expansion of the soul, adrift between flashes of enlightenment and sweetly perfumed intuitions. Acting as something of a priest, moreover, D'Ambra would administer to a small band of initiates a secret rite that bordered on heresy by appearing to claim the monopoly of a rarefied body of knowledge beyond the reach of logical systems. A fanatical collector of a confused botanical and pharmacological bric-à-brac, in tune with seventeenth-century taste, this Florentine dandy

a thousand scents inventeth . . . ,
With fans and small upholstery;
He makes very sweet perfumes,
And fumigations for your rooms;
He makes powderets,
He makes odorets
And all for certain marvellously;
. . . from the summits of Peru,
From the forests of Tolù
Let him lay
(I'll be bold to say)
A thousand drugs in, and more too.[2]

Such a man would hardly have felt at ease in the *cabinet* of an up-to-the-minute philosopher. After all, the mystique of smells had arisen as a weak and subtle backlash of snobbery against the new science with its all-embracing geometricalization of the cosmos. Even human consciousness was now an object of investigation by the impassive logic of numbers and the icy and odourless geometry of shapes. There could be no foothold for odorous mysticism in eighteenth-century salons dedicated to the cult of physics and the exact sciences, nor could it entertain any hope of survival in a cultural environment in which the indiscretion of smells and olfactory espionage constituted a grave affront to privacy. For to protect the private domain there was a screen of contrived and measured mathematical sensitivity that was engaged in caressing elegant and multicoloured shapes, both soft and blurred, further refined through the use of graceful and miniaturized proportions. This was the equivalent, in another context, of a shift from the superlative to the diminutive, from hyperbole to reasonableness.

But this gentleman with his alembic and his undying devotion to the retort, busying himself with the distillation of smells and the selection of flavours in a state of perfect equilibrium between the poles of nose and mouth, represented the last example of a seventeenth-century creature doomed to extinction. Of tone-coloured and polychrome cuisine, visualized and divided into sections, juxtaposed but never amalgamated, of the eighteenth-century cuisine of the gaze, D'Ambra knew nothing at all.

> Thus continually joking and jovial, he is
> The very quintessence of olfactory science.
> He is so very learned that even when he
> Sneezes, it as if his nose had passed a sentence
> That the 'odourists', at their tribunal,
> Must record when they meet at conference,
> Where they are addressed by the greatest of greedy-guts
> Of whom Magalotti is the supreme patriarch.
>
> Nor without this flower of gluttony
> Could this nasal authentication ever take place,
> Since the mouth and the nose have always
> Worked in concert, whether for good or for evil;
> And it seems that the agreement between them is
> That taste and scent are only valid
> If what one puts in one's mouth smells good to the nose
> And if one's mouth judges good what the nose also likes.
>
> So, his science of scents keeps close company
> With his science of tastes, which is fine and perfect,
> And he has his recipes fetched from the land of honey
> By special delivery or personal courier;
> And he spares neither expense nor trouble
> To put all these recipes to the severest of tests.[3]

Yet the great Knight of the Accademia degli Odoristi of Tuscany, 'who were forever shuffling recipes belonging to the Infanta Isabella or to Don Florenzo of Ullhoa . . . and who scorned every fragrance that was not strange, composite and exquisite',[4] none the less foreshadowed the eighteenth-century craze for chinoiserie, for both oriental and tropical exoticism, the taste for porcelain, for knick-knacks, furnishings and miscellaneous salon ironmongery imported from faraway Cathay or even further away Chipangu.

D'Ambra's omnivorous passion for collection and his inquisitive science, a relic of seventeenth-century hoarding gigantism, had driven him to cram all available wonders from the West and the East Indies into a late baroque *Wunderkammer* that had not yet been turned into a *cabinet* devoted to natural history.[5] This was in perfect keeping with the architecture of his overblown warehouse-palace in which the delicate Florentine 'manner' was forced to cohabit, in strident *mésalliance*, with exotic barbarism, and where 'to judge by the pomp and ceremony / One might be expecting a Pope in each room'.

> And with his high imperial ways
> He is not only triumphant in Tuscany
> But has rendered even the Indies genial,
> Which range from China to Peru:
> And from their gifts, artificial or natural,
> With his own hands he has created a cabinet
> Unique in the world for its gems and its gold
> The great Mogor alone possesses one that is larger.
>
> And all the rest of his quarter, like a royal
> Palace, wherein both Barbarian and Tuscan
> Styles of architecture are confused,
> Is similar to his cabinet,
> And keep hidden both Brazil and Japan:
> But it is a Roman-style Japan and Brazil
> Where, to judge by all the pomp and ceremony,
> One might be expecting a Pope in each room.[6]

In his storehouse of marvels the sophisticated lover of botanical treasures and other curiosities had assembled 'the rarest plants which each of the Indies contains'.

> Let us add to this a thousand perfume waters
> A thousand flowers, all of them extravagant,
> All with new scents, with original colours,
> And so many soils in which to plant them
> And all brought back from distant countries
> From South, from North, from West, from East
> There is even earth from distant Tonkin
> That turns a rosy hue to golden brown.[7]

Flowers, perfumed tannins, herbs, soils, trees with names so barbarous that 'if you want to cure the possessed / Without any other exorcizing ointment, / It is enough just to name the trees / That make the sceptres of the Indian crowns':[8]

> Iraperanga, sercandam, bamboo,
> Totake, rametul, coatl, chaoba,
> Tunal, tamalapatra, araticù,
> Cacakuaquahuitl, hacchio, bacoba,
> Calampart, anda, munduyquacù
> (Just imagine the devil withstanding that)
> Baobat, ietaiba, quaichtlepopotl,
> Bonduch, arecca, acajarba, achiotl.[9]

Cocoa, tobacco, red pepper, quinquina, coca . . . Europe's botanical and pharmaceutical treasure-house was ballooning. Over every other smell fanatic there towered the kingly figure of the 'terrible Count', the 'arduous Magalotti / Patriarch of satraps and gluttons'.

> An emphatic speech
> An ecstatic mind
> Knowledge greater than any grand grammarian
> The wish to clamber higher than a dozen Nimrods:
> Such is the massive Magalotti.[10]

'On the occasion of the *stravizzo* of the thirteenth day of September in the year 1699' Lorenzo Bellini delivered a *cicalata* before the Accademia della Crusca – a *cicalata* being an elegant speech on a strange or meaningless topic and a *stravizzo* the solemn dinner at which a *cicalata* was generally delivered. In Bellini's *cicalata* Magalotti, the 'hero of the nose', admitted to being but 'a poor table musketeer (except in certain trifles, the strongest of which is in smells, so that rather than call them dishes, one might, by introversion, call them flavours)'.[11] In Bellini's account the great lover of perfumes, whom the Accademia della Crusca knew as the 'Lofty', pontificated like a gentle despot and took under his wing the *cicalatore* of the evening, the madcap anatomist and author of *La buchereide* (a comic poem about the popular infatuation for *buccheri*), Lorenzo Bellini himself.

He is that fine article of your academic furniture, that great Satrap made entirely of mind and a mind made entirely of segments of oracle flesh, and mystery entrails, mixed and packed with world-seed emulations and idea-marrows, your Great Lofty, to whose goodness, therefore, and not to myself, you must know yourself to be indebted for having this evening someone to entertain you; he sought him out in the land of Gog and Magog thanks to these countless correspondences that he has with the whales of the North and with the falsettos of Nangan; and he wants yet more; he wants me to ask you on his behalf to hold in some quite distinct consideration the orator that you will see in this pulpit.[12]

But beneath the academician's wig there protruded a nose whose 'nervous papillae, with which the entire surface of the sensory organ is, as it were, studded and sprinkled', produced a 'constant tickling of the senses'. This functioned as a kind of 'spiritual fumigation' on a monstrously prehensile brain capable of raising itself from odorous essences towards heavenly metaphysics. Behind 'these great, beautiful and jovial cheeks, doused with barley beer, fertilized and crammed with butter' (as Francesco Redi wrote facetiously, sending him 'a thousand highly perfumed kisses'),[13] there hid a 'mind utterly dedicated to exquisite perfection in all its operations':

> right down to humble and small matters he was Lofty, and great. Just look at him, plunged in smells, handling flowers and *buccheri* and performing strong-smelling manipulations, and in other guises, as some would madly judge him, wasting his time . . . Never did he stoop to humble things, but rather rendered them sublime. In the same way, our Lofty magnified what was small, raised up what was low, made noble what was vile and, since he had the purest of tastes, carried everything to exquisite perfection. What seemed to the ignorant plebs to be excessive sweetness and delicacy was only his longing for perfection.[14]

An intransigent mystagogue of this 'voluptuous liturgy' of smells, Magalotti had managed to ensure that even the roughest and rudest of his servants, those who could barely distinguish thyme from rosemary, little by little became the most careful of examiners of the most delicate of concoctions, skilled at manipulating, inventing, altering, making discoveries and nosing out, not the classics of perfumery, amber, musk and civet, which is very easy, but flowers and citrus fruits, roots and herbs, agallochs and *zidre*, *ciaccherandà*, calambacs, eagle-wood, alabasters, gums, *rage*, *tracantidi*, balsams, *animi*, quinine, clays, *buccheri* and very many others.

> *Unhinged and startling names that might*
> *Frighten the dead in the graveyards at night.*[15]

THIRTEEN

QUINTESSENCES OF JUICES

In the 'great halls' of 'golden-roofed' palaces[1] the eighteenth-century table, 'sparkling with fine silverware / and foreign ceramics, exhibits and dispenses / its noble and considered flavours'.[2] Such fine and subtle tastes were planned and developed to match the style of a well-ordered and measured cuisine, custom-made for effervescent and witty table companions, highly-strung 'foppish dandies'[3] and ethereal ladies flitting, at the rhythm and speed of the latest body-language, between silverware, high-class trinketry and diaphanous porcelain that, by its very fragility, appeared to express the same *esprit de finesse* as the hands that caressed it. Delicate porcelain of 'Saxon clay', 'by means of which Europe has defeated Chinese art',[4] bowls, tea-pots, coffee-pots, 'soup plates and dinner plates', enamel work and miniatures, sorbet and chocolate makers, fine furnishings and decorations, all became an integral part of the general dinner performance, a visual earnest of the precious and tasty delights to come, and pointers on the 'quest for happiness'.

In the dazzling halls where the light of a thousand candles reflected by 'precisely cut crystals' bounced off softly tinted cream or pistachio walls

> the fine ladies beautifully enwrapped
> by the opulent flourishes of their finery
> are welcomed among the attentive knights
> bathing in the elegant flower of their youth;

> and now, attending to noble games,
> they repose on soft and easy chairs;
> and now, they weave nocturnal dances
> beneath the brilliance of sparkling glass.[5]

Meals were becoming vaguely imaginary, an elegantly conventional appendage to social rituals whose highpoints occurred in other venues and at other times. There were other kinds of blandishment for stoking desire, other kinds of pleasure for sating the appetite, other forms of seduction emanating from the graceful pseudo-oriental interiors where ladies 'might, if they please, Savour the juice / Of Indian fruit in a Chinese bowl'.[6] Spread out on the tables, yet further temptations emitted their voluptuous and irresistible messages:

> Some people drink Mexican chocolate
> which is already steaming and odorous;
> others the tender and frozen ambrosia
> of sorbet, coloured by strawberry;
> yet others the fiery liquor born of the vine
> or of Hesperus' kingdom, or of the dawn;
> but if you listen to me you'll take Egyptian coffee
> and that placid Chinese herb, tea.[7]

Gallant high society was attended upon by the delicacies of the buffet and the refinements of the dessert.

Plates had grown smaller now that modern diners craved 'very delicious small dishes',[8] 'pâtés' and 'quintessences of juices'[9] and had abandoned the 'ancient manner',[10] the outmoded baroque style whereby 'one ate with plentiful liberality which comforted the sitting diner, who would eat his full, freed of any fear of depriving a prize titbit if not from his table companion's fork then perhaps from his longing eye'.[11] The new 'Sybarites'[12] 'rich voluptuaries who had in some cases lost and, as it were, worn out their taste by dint of using it, therefore require the energy of sauces and consommés made from every type of meat in order to avoid the trouble of actually doing any chewing'.[13] One old feudal lord, feeling nostalgic for the bygone years of baroque grandeur, complained:

> At meals that are said to be magnificent, there is an infinite range of saucers and small crockery, but they hold so wretchedly little that one can hardly get a mouthful of food from each dish . . . Some houses, since the fashion for banquets began, have slimmed down their ordinarily meagre fare, while piling praise on healthy simplicity. If, despite everything, a certain air of ceremony is maintained, there is always what is called 'the weekly pie', thus named because it has to last the whole week through: this is what Madame de Maintenon, in one of her famous letters to Madame d'Aubigné, referred to as the 'pyramide éternelle'.[14]

There is no need to take the noble lord's nostalgic complaints about feudal meals too literally or to believe that 'healthy simplicity' really did verge on starvation. In the eighteenth century those who wished to and could afford to still ate in magnificent abundance.

Certainly there is no point mentioning the 'dishes of sovereigns and Gods'.[15] If one is to believe 'Monsieur Mercier', who maintained that in France people had only found out 'how to eat in the last fifty years',[16] Louis XIV, during his interminable reign, never once tried Gascon *garbure* (cabbage soup), even though he suffered under neither financial nor dietary constraints. Frederick the Great, however, an enlightened and cultivated prince *par excellence*, who had even composed verses in praise of *pâté à la sardanapale*, recommended to him by his chief steward, liked on occasion to remain at table for a full three hours. The evening before such occasions, however, he would order 'the victuals (of a limited number moreover) from cooks of different nations'[17] and he would himself propose 'recommendations and experiments'.[18] A thorough cosmopolitan, as well as a Prussian, Frederick was an outstanding strategist even when it came to cuisine, admirable for an internationalism that was free from even the slightest hint of culinary chauvinism.

In the eighteenth century 'noble banquets'[19] (*stravizzi*) were still a widespread practice, though the rich principally craved 'refinement, novelty and variety'.[20]

Contemporary documents are full of fabulous and invasive parasites, or *cicisbei of the teeth*, as Carlo Innocenzo Frugoni, a poet familiar with the most opulent tables of Bologna and Parma, called them. In Milan Prince Tolomeo Trivulzio, the well-deserving founder of the Charitable institution homonym (Pietro Verri mentions it in a letter written in 1770), since he was a true 'Lombard Sardanapalian',

> had the chickens educated for several months, first purging them, and then filling them with strong-smelling herbs and cooked vegetables. He was a man who would feed a bullock for two years or more on nothing but pure milk, in order to produce divinely succulent meat. He would fry the eggs in the fat of garden warblers! This is our Newton, and he is not the only Milanese of this type,
>
> *For ancient valour*
> *Is not yet extinguished in Italian hearts.*[21]

In 'matters edible' Rome and Naples, with all their devotees of antiquity, hellenists, neoclassicist aesthetes and idealistic dreamers, could not, in Pietro Verri's view, experience to the full the 'delights of the soft palate'. After all, Verri went on, 'this is an absolutely Gallic skill, practised throughout the whole of Gaul'. So at least as far as cookery was concerned, a return to the ways of the ancients could bring only illusions and disappointment.

> I do not know if it is true that the Prince of San Severo, at Naples, one day decided to give a dinner served in the ancient style and prepared strictly in accordance with the precepts of Petronius, Horace, etc., and that at the end of the meal all the lovers of antiquity rose from the table still famished.[22]

Luckily, Raimondo di Sangro, the alchemist prince who was said to have discovered the formula for producing artificial blood, had the good taste to confine himself to classical experiments rather than allowing himself to be tempted by the kind of extravagant culinary exploits embarked upon by emperors of the Late Roman Empire such as Heliogabalus who, as eighteenth-century gastronomic archaeology was now discovering,

> being quite excessively self-indulgent in all things, on certain days ordered an entire dinner to be prepared using nothing but vegetables, on other days nothing but fruit, on yet others nothing but sweet and honeyed dishes, and sometimes dishes all made from milk. He had skilled buffet experts so highly trained in the art of manipulating sweetmeats and dairy products that they could produce marvellous imitations, with milk and honey, of all the dishes the cooks normally make with meat, fish and many other sorts of animals. They also knew how to counterfeit every kind of fruit in a thousand different ways.[23]

It was a time when, in the wake of the Renaissance, erudite attention was refocusing on the table rituals of the ancients. This was in perfect synchrony with the archaeological discoveries in Rome and, in particular, in Herculaneum and with the widespread passion for 'ancient curiosities' and Roman and Greek remains.

In Florence the *Lezioni toscane* on the *Conviti pubblici de' Romani, e della loro magnificenza* (Public banquets of the Romans and their magnificence) by Giuseppe Averani, a member of the Accademia della Crusca, were republished in 1766. To some extent Averani's *Lezioni* had been prefigured in the 'erudite entertainment' *Dell'uso delle ghirlande e degli unguenti ne'conviti degli antichi* (Ferrara, 1698), by Giuseppe Lanzoni, a Ferrarese doctor and friend of Francesco Redi. But while Florentines once again perused Averani's *Lezioni*, in Rome Winckelmann and Mengs were engaged in an attempt to rediscover and reinterpret classical antiquity. Yet in that Rome of Clement XIII, during the Carnival season,'castrati dressed up like princesses' with 'languid glances and amorous actions' drove the Roman priests mad, tormenting them with indecent passions 'for these Antinouses'.[24]

Alessandro Verri, meanwhile, caught between passions, between a leisurely stroll and a gallant dinner, had much greater opportunity to devote himself to the study of Greek than the effeminate young Prussian who, being 'extremely busy from morning until evening', wrote in a halting mixture of Latin and Italian: 'I am eating bread that I have earned by the sweat of my brow, and especially on Saturday when I have to cook.'[25] However, when Giacomo Casanova invited him to dinner, Winckelmann found the occasion provided him with a welcome rest from his long hours grappling with antiquity and subject to Hellenizing fevers, especially after a few bottles of Orvieto, his favourite wine. Winckelmann was no doubt a more sophisticated and agreeable eating companion than Anton Raphael Mengs, an associate of Winckelmann in the pursuit of the beautiful. In the privacy of his home Mengs forgot the 'principles' pertaining to fine art and got drunk every day and often brutally humiliated his wife, the beautiful Margherita Guazzi de Mengs, whom he had once shared, in a spirit of true comradeship, with his Prussian colleague. Winckelmann, the sensitive 'doctor umbraticus', ended his life in an inn in Trieste, his throat slit by a handsome street-walking fop. Giacomo Casanova described Mengs as 'obstinate and cruel', a man who 'when at home, always rose from the table drunk: but away from home drank only water'. After the monumental achievements of Montfaucon and the Count of Caylus, archaeology had turned into a great collective fever that was eagerly devouring cultivated Europe. One day in Rome in 1775 Abbot Etienne Bonnot de Condillac, who was, besides, a 'good table companion', 'on considering the fact that no one invited him to lunch and that everyone showed him statues, could not prevent himself from exclaiming: what a beautiful country if only one could eat statues!'[26]

Pietro Leopoldo I, Grand Duke of Tuscany, was given a very different reception on his arrival in Rome in 1769. Although he was an 'extreme' lover of antiquity, instead of presenting him with 'archaeological rarities', the conclave sent him 'one hundred and thirty porters bearing goods; mostly edible: hams, ratafias, brandy, mortadella, coffee, chocolate, confectionery; two live calves, a fragment of the Holy Cross, tied in gold, and so on. It looked like the march of Iarba, King of the Moors. The porters were extraordinarily tattered and were falling to pieces.'[27]

In Rome, despite widespread and seething passions for antiquity, the convivial traditions of the great houses and of prelates' love feasts lived on. Cardinal Domenico Passionei, 'the pasha of Fossombrone', the chief librarian of the Vatican Library and a sophisticated bibliophile, was an implacable foe of the Jesuits but a friend of Giacomo Casanova and a protector of Johann Joachim Winckelmann. In the gold-decorated suburban retreat that he called 'Camaldoli', in reference to the Camaldolite order,

> on the hills of Rome, when he removed his red hat to don a light straw one, he would refer to his holiday companions as 'Friar this and Friar that' and to their rooms as 'cells'. Yet in actual fact these friars went neither to the chancel to sing tunes, nor to the refectory to eat vegetables and omelettes. The forests of Brazil, the pagodas of China, bottles of wine from the Cape of Good Hope, partridge *pâtés* from Périgord: these were the only ideas that could excite this voluptuous monasticism.[28]

Pope Ganganelli, by contrast, a former Capuchin friar and anti-Jesuit, a man whom Passionei referred to in public as a 'coglione' (literally, a 'testicle'), eventually decided to have his 'domestic life' depicted in fresco on the walls of Castelgandolfo. Despite his austere table discipline, the Pope wished to be portrayed 'in white riding clothes', galloping 'on horseback, followed by some of his baser retinue of cooks, assistant cooks, kitchen boys and cleaners, all of whom were instantly recognizable as the people whom he kept close to him'. Elsewhere one might admire 'His Holiness going for a walk and, not far away, a kitchen boy of the court, known as "seven-pastas", famous for the favour showered upon him by the Pope, from whom he had obtained this delightful name'.[29] It was a strange kind of evangelical riding party that depicted the Vicar of Christ, surrounded by his court of skivvies, kitchen boys, cleaners and cooks, and a peculiar papal scene that captured the Prince of Rome on a secret stroll with his simple (or not so simple) kitchen lad. It seemed a spectacular overturning of hierarchy, a dazzling allegory of dethronement and of humility made flesh. Sadly, all such familiarity with his devoted kitchen brigade did nothing to save him from the poison which (it was said) was administered to him on the orders of the Jesuits.

In the great princely palaces, like that of the Ruspoli, certain evening entertainments assumed a high-class and neoclassical style. At a reception given in honour of the Archduke of Austria in 1775, following the course of the Berbers,

> we were led ... into a gallery where there was a table for at least one hundred persons, fully laid with ice-creams and a dessert in the form of huge banks, temples, gardens, porcelain statues, all of which was magnificent and opulent. We then went down to ground floor and entered a well-decorated ballroom, which corresponded to the recently arranged and well-lit garden. Against the side of the ballroom leaned a pergola decorated with statues, which, by way of a few steps, led down into the garden. Opposite was Mount Parnassus with Apollo and the nine Muses and Pegasus beating his hoof, beneath which spouted the fountain of Hippocrene. On the other two sides, on oak trunks arranged to form a colonnade, there were two orchestras. All the bowls of citrus fruits were lit up by lights hidden inside large hollowed-out lemons, so that their light shone through the thin rind. Under the orchestras there were two other fountains decorated with statues. The aisles of the orchestra were of multicoloured sand mixed with sparkling glass powder. At the top and all the way round, the scene was completed by a green bower, decorated with statues. Everything was artificial, including the statues which were made of pasteboard and the fountains that were specially designed for the occasion.[30]

In 1774, in the house of the Imbonati in Milan, at a soirée of truly Roman grandeur given by Prince Chigi, the walls were hung with 'decorations all taken from ancient Herculaneum'. 'There was no less magnificence and elegance in the mirrors, painted canvases, false vaults, floors covered with green sheeting or buffets made to look like theatre sets.

> Each lady received a magnificent bouquet of flowers, then oranges, then exquisite refreshments that kept on circulating ... Towards midnight the buffet appeared. Without making a sound, two large

tables were set in the first hall with at least twenty other smaller tables around them. The available space decreased, and yet it was incredible to note the foresight that our host and his servants had used to arrange every detail. The various princes and ladies took their places and everyone who wanted to do so did likewise at the other tables. The profusion of sea fish, sea food, truffles, pheasant, partridge, etc. and of wines was surprising: so many offerings overwhelmed me. I saw some rather indiscreet eaters, not far away, who were stuffing themselves with oysters. Then Tokay and then the same again. When the dinner was finished, everything vanished quickly and a new table was laid with equal refinement, and the second was followed by a third so that, when the feast and the night both came to an end, the leftovers of all this gluttony were enough to provide the musicians with a sumptuous meal. They said that Chigi had spent more than 6,000 sequins.[31]

The lighting – as Pietro Verri commented – was 'grandiose'. As day broke and the lights were put out (it was 16 February), the multiple and seemingly interminable feast at last drew to a close.

FOURTEEN

THE LAVISH TABLE

The Italian provinces had scarcely been touched by the delicacies that resulted from the new intellectual trends and by the elegant magnificence of aristocratic salons. North of the Po the moderation that reformers preached was quite unknown. Ordinary fare remained essentially unchanged right into the second half of the eighteenth century. In the duchy of Parma and Piacenza, for example, a typical meal at a local tavern at the end of the eighteenth century would not have been very different from the fixed-price meal served in the first decade of the century to G. B. Labat, a Dominican friar. Having dismounted from his horse at an inn in Borgo San Donnino, Friar Labat was brought

> a pea soup, a stew, calf sweetbreads and a large roast pigeon. The innkeeper came to see me and ordered me a ham. He encouraged me to drink and eat. Then I had artichokes with salt and pepper, then strawberries and excellent cheese, with chilled white and red wine.[1]

With the exception of snow-chilled wine, which was a traditional seventeenth-century speciality, the basic meal in northern Italy – right into the nineteenth century – still consisted of some kind of soup, a stew, a dish of something fried and one of something roasted.

In many cities the culinary reforms ushered in by the Enlightenment encountered stubborn resistance and blank rejection among the most elevated social groupings. 'Lavish eating' merrily outlived every reform and every fashion – at least among men. In Bologna Giampietro Zanotti, a member of the Accademia Clementina and a theoretician of beauty in painting, a man whom Abbot Roberti often found 'slumbering at the hearthside in his spacious and well-lit kitchen',[2] calmly ignored the gastronomic reforms. He managed none the less to live to over ninety without renouncing the ancient pleasures of a lavish and tasty dinner-table. Roberti remembered Zanotti as

> a strong and very corpulent man, with an outstanding appetite . . . He was a great eater of dishes that were both good and substantial, like a choice hunk of juicy beef. I remember that once, seated beside him at table, I offered him, with all the courtesy in which I prided myself, a warbler or perhaps a bunting. And he, on turning it down, replied that he did not enjoy anything smaller than quail, but that as for bigger birds, he would happily tackle an eagle.
>
> In the scale of fowl and edible creatures, he considered that chickens raised with love at home by one's stewards, ducks well fed in the miller's yard and heavy and meaty-breasted guinea-hens were to be eaten on the most festive days of the Carnival. His Most Reverend Monsignor Vitaliano Borromée, the Vice-Legate of Bologna and now the Emeritus Cardinal of the Holy Church, said jokingly to me one day that he did not wish Giampietro Zanotti to dine with him again because Zanotti had had the temerity to praise a capon at his table and had displayed insufficient appreciation for a certain orange-coloured sauce (which we Italian mortals would call a 'yellow stock'), a sauce, moreover, so famous and exquisite that in Paris its preparation is part of the examination to become a cook.[3]

The insensitivity that this distinguished Bolognese (born in Paris in 1674 and, moreover, of a Parisian mother) displayed towards French sauces reveals the deep-seated refusal and the ancestral rejection with which traditional-minded people encountered the influx of new food fashions from across the Alps. The episode recounted by Father Roberti also makes it easier to gauge the difference between the table of the Vice-Legate of Bologna and the doubtless more modest table of the bishopric of Imola. A few decades later, in the days of the Benedictine bishop Barnabas Chiaramonti (before he was elected Pope at a difficult time for the papacy), the latter table appeared stubbornly opposed to all those imported sauces (except béchamel) that, according to cosmopolitan and French-trained chefs, constituted the 'foundations of good cookery'. 'A tasty and delicate sauce is the soul of any excellent food,'[4] pronounced Francesco Leonardi. Sauces were all the better if they had been enhanced with champagne: 'if this is used in the place of ordinary wine, not only sauces but every kind of food gains a more exquisite and delicate flavour'.[5] It appears, however, that Alberto Alvisi, chef to the Bishop of Imola, did not follow the same precepts, preferring to make exclusive use of 'sweet and generous wine'[6] and the local Sangiovese, known for its violet-scented bouquet. The Bishop of Imola's cuisine was indeed provincial, strongly attached to the old Romagnole tradition and to the handing down of the oral knowledge accumulated by the old patriarchal houses of the ancient Exarchate. It could be a mere coincidence, but there is no mention of chocolate anywhere in the papers left us by Alvisi. Nor does chocolate ever make any appearance, either in solid or in liquid form, in the buffet of Barnabas Chiaramonti. Perhaps, out of loyalty to the Benedictine tradition, Bishop Chiaramonti simply wanted to steer clear of such an alluring sweet so intricately linked to the order of St Ignatius. In the meantime, however, Loyola's hard-working successors were spreading chocolate far and wide, securing a monopoly control over its trade and distribution and using it (as their many enemies kept saying) as part of a political strategy, for the greater glory of the Omnipotent and of his Society. No Jesuit's house was free of the delicate scent of cocoa. But the profane world also took to it with rapture. Pietro Verri liked his chocolate very, indeed excessively, sweet. His brother Alessandro teasingly reminded him of his preference for 'good, yet vanilla-free' Roman chocolate, saying, 'I remember that that is how you like it, from pure depravity.'[7] And so from Milan, his enlightened brother would keep him well supplied. In 1772, writing from Rome, Alessandro thanked his brother: 'at last I have received the wine, chocolate and papers . . . The chocolate is exquisite. The cocoa is all from Caracas and the vanilla is perfect. They do not make any chocolate in Rome that is this good.'[8] In Bologna Pier Iacopo Martello, who in 'Lo starnuto di Ercole' (The sneeze of Hercules) criticized the French mania 'for maintaining the order and arrangement of their foods, whether it be their fragrant soups or their pyramid-shaped desserts',[9] displayed his fascination in 'Il vero parigino italiano' (The true Parisian Italian) for 'Indian broth, which I like so much and which more than anything else generates outlandish thoughts in my head'.[10]

Father Roberti, whom the Piedmontese count Benvenuto di San Rafaele described as a 'placid and joyous Jesuit'[11] and as a 'plain rough fellow', described himself, somewhat over-modestly, as a 'simple man of letters'. Roberti cast an ironic gaze on those 'sophisticated literary people' who 'strive nowadays to achieve a level of delicate mobility in their nervous system, since, in their view, this was a sign of a lively and agile wit' free of the 'migraines, hypochondria, vapours and convulsions' that were 'especially attendant on fine minds'. Indeed, when such a wit sought inspiration, he would never call on either Apollo or the Muses but instead consume 'a bowl of chocolate or more often of coffee'.[12]

While in Bologna (he remained there almost a quarter of a century, until the day when the Jesuits were flushed out *manu militari* from the College of Santa Lucia), Father Roberti received in his 'little room' 'Dr Francesco Zanotti':

> to this poet, to this philosopher, to this divine author I offered a large bowl full of chocolate; on the table there was an elegant sweet dish bearing loaves resembling Spanish bread but rather better, made in Venice by the hands of maidens, and as yellow as the gold from the Venice Mint, broad, big, soft, spongy, delicious. The Crusca does not help me to describe and define them properly: here we call them *savoyards*, and if they are thus called because they do in fact originate in Savoy, I would thank Monsieur le Comte [Knight Benvenuto Robbio, Count of San Rafaele, to whom the letter was addressed] for the sweet and delicious cakes that his Savoy sends us.

The old man, breaking his fast, having already sucked the head of froth from the top of the bowl, dipped his savoyard in the thick and gentle drink, well suited to the teeth that he lacked. But the cake, being spongy, immediately soaked up all the liquid so that softened and fragile lumps fell into the drink and had to be fished out again, or rather quickly sucked out, though by that time they had already turned to mush. Then my good Zanotti would turn towards me, his lips not indecorously dirty and, with friendly and serene eyes, he would say in a pitiable manner: 'Father Roberti, you see my misfortune: this dear but impertinent savoyard longed to become soup and has gulped down my entire bowl of chocolate.' The *chocolatière* was still boiling and steaming so that these disagreements between a sweet biscuit and a man of the law were calmed the instant I poured him out a fresh bowlful. Then he would begin to drink, having finished eating. It was then that our little dialogues would begin. I remained standing, attentive, and whenever the chocolate seemed close to the bottom of the bowl, I would pour more in to top it right up, after a brief and friendly objection on his part. We called this latter treat – our term for it was very accurate – the *little contentment*. Indeed, in the name of one of my unerring customs, I never allowed anyone to leave my chamber unhappy on this account. The distinguished old man, following this plentiful treat, his mind revived and reinvigorated, fired off sallies and quibbles with quick wit and pleasure.[13]

This provides an elegant tableau of comfortable Bolognese life in former times, a sketch of private surroundings painted in the delicate shades suggested by the nostalgic and emotionally charged memory of a blameless exile. Father Roberti in fact wrote the above from Bassano in 1786, after he had been forced to leave the civilized and cultured city of Bologna.

Father Roberti insisted on chocolate of quality: although a lover of 'dark chocolate' (according to Clemente Bondi), he was not unfamiliar with Soconosco cocoa, the 'very lightest-coloured kind of chocolate',[14] preferred by the courts. 'Once,' he recalled, 'I too had a 6-pound sample of chocolate made with this very select cocoa, given to me by a cordon bleu chef, Count Jacopo Sanvitali, butler to the Duchess of Parma, who was also the eldest daughter of the King of France. In Rome His Eminent Royal Highness, Cardinal of York, had delivered to my room 30 pounds of chocolate, a substance that he, a man who confined himself to eating vegetables, drank in the mornings.'[15] Yet it is unlikely that this vegetarian Prince of the Church drank 30 pounds of chocolate every morning, as some interpreters have argued.

For many years Mexican 'nectar' was a constant fixture at the 'morning meal' of Count Roberti who, as he said himself, treated himself 'royally'.

Yet initially the 'Indian nut' 'selected for a noble and lucky usage' and transformed into an 'agreeable drink'[16] aroused considerable suspicion and concern among the inhabitants of Europe.

> Some people believed that it was a condensed animal jelly whose taste was imparted by various strong-smelling ingredients. Others thought it was a pie containing exotic mushrooms or fucus seaweed. The more perspicacious deemed it to be a herbal extract or something derived from the bark of aromatic trees from the Indies . . .
>
> The opinions of the first Europeans to land on the shores of northern America, as regards the strengths and drawbacks of this exotic drink, were no less discordant. Some, having tasted it and tried it out, praised it too highly, deeming it a delicious tonic particularly well suited to the sustenance of weak constitutions. Others, while erudite, although, quite astonishingly, they refused to taste it, condemned it out of hand as a barbarous invention that was unworthy to pass the lips of any European. This view was adopted most notably by two very renowned men of letters of this era: Girolamo Benzoni, from Milan, who accompanied the Spanish on their first expeditions; and the naturalist Giuseppe Acosta, who visited Mexico not long thereafter. Benzoni, in his history of the New World, published in 1572, even dared to say that cocoa was a drink fit more for pigs than for men. And Acosta, in his *Istoria morale e naturale dell'Indie*, remarked that the Spanish who had settled in Mexico loved chocolate to the point of madness; but that one had to grow accustomed to the drink in order to overcome the feeling of nausea at the very sight of the froth that swam on top, like the scum floating on top of a fermented liqueur. He concluded that it was nothing more nor less than a Mexican superstition, for in those days the uses and customs of Americans were considered generally to be superstitious.

Yet the ever active and ingenious spirit of commerce quickly found a way to allay all such prejudices and successfully introduced cocoa and the use of chocolate into Europe. The highest-ranking classes and the monarchs themselves were pleased to substitute the new drink in the place of their previous beverages.[17]

The American Jesuit abbot Gioan-Ignazio Molina, member of the Institute of Sciences of Bologna, wrote:

> According to my observations, the chocolate that is commonly manufactured in Italy far surpasses that which is made in any other place both in its taste and in its healthfulness. It is nutritional, it fortifies the stomach, it is easily digested, it acts quickly to revive flagging strength, it strengthens the nervous system and it is well suited to sustaining decrepit old age.[18]

Their severe shortage of chocolate notwithstanding, the doctors of Bologna also treated themselves 'royally' – Francesco Maria Zanotti, Giampietro's brother, was director of the famous Institute of Sciences. These learned men, vaccinated, as it were, by the 'lavish table', did not suffer from 'migraines, pallors or indigestion combined with mild convulsions', syndromes that were typical of the 'honourable sicknesses which, according to Tissot, are peculiar to sedentary and contemplative men of letters'.[19] Abbot Roberti, proudly loyal to Italian traditions, even culinary ones, was fond of stressing that 'the people of Paris are the worst-fed people anywhere in Europe'. He went even further, adding that

> the faddishness of some Frenchmen is so arrogant that, when they arrive in Italy, as soon as they taste one of our dishes prepared in a manner different from that which is customary on the other side of their Alps, even if they are only poor men (ballet teachers or language teachers, for example), yet do they decide that the dish before them is utterly detestable.[20]

Reacting firmly against the 'great palaces devoid of jubilation, / Vainly proud of their golden roofs', against the delights of their refined and sophisticated tables, Clemente Bondi, in 'L'asinata' (or 'La giornata villereccia'), also displayed annoyance:

> What do I care if a Gallic chef,
> With expert art, colours my dishes,
> And if, with peculiar wit, he teaches
> My food to tell lies with sweet tastes?
> What do I care if pomp-crazy tables are decked
> With Dresden china or sculpted silverware,
> And if from over the mountains and seas
> An unknown vine sends us the choicest of wine?[21]

Far from the fine palaces, in the 'blessed villa', a meal 'of not much expense' and without 'luxury', consumed 'in a humble abode', would have sufficed to restore lost appetite, especially if the 'pastoral banquet' included polenta garnished with skylarks, woodcocks and warblers:

> Long ignored, it remained an abhorred bait
> Alone in the villages, base and abandoned;
> And banished from every noble table
> Food fit only for coarse humble folk;
> Later, better seasoned, accepted
> In towns and among civilized people,
> It managed at last to arouse
> The delicate desires of fine ladies and knights.[22]

To people of delicate constitution and a weak stomach such peasant food seemed to be a form of medical treatment. 'For the last few days,' Algarotti wrote to Abbot Bettinelli in 1753, 'I am recovering my health thanks to polenta taken on an empty stomach: it has become my chocolate.'[23]

In stark opposition to 'French gluttony',[24] Italian polenta was able to set itself up as a powerful vaccine, as were the Italian-style meals that were served in Rome at the house of Cardinal Corsini:

> Woodcocks, partridges and francolins,
> Thrushes that looked as if made of wax,
> Pullets and tender young pigeons
> Were piled in high mounds; just like
> The Carnival evening at Casa Corsini.
> There were pastries of every description.

Wines I won't speak of: they were all there.
Sweet, full-bodied, dry and mellow.[25]

The holy kitchens of the Vatican were centres of culinary traditionalism that had been left almost untouched by modernity. Yet even during obligatory fasts, on the eve of solemn feasts, they managed to earn the admiration of such demanding observers as President de Brosses, who spent several months in the Rome of Clement XII between 1739 and 1740. His sophisticated antiquarian's eye rested for a long time on the violet dinner (it was Christmas Eve of 1739 and the Church was displaying the colours of Advent) given by the Pope in the royal hall of the Quirinale, following a concert and an oratorio. The guests were served

> a splendid collation which, even in the view of the Abbot of Périgny, might be termed a good supper. A long, rather narrow table had been laid with a line of decorative tableware, pleasantly fashioned out of ice-cream, artificial flowers and fruit, flanked by two other lines of large pieces, whether real or imitation, of lettuces, vegetables, jams, compotes, etc.; everything serving the almost exclusive purpose of representation and of forming a permanent service: this was the splendid collation. The following was the good supper: a great architricline, in a violet cassock on account of Advent, standing at the head of the table, performed the function of serving the food, which the lower-ranking waiters, as violet as he, placed on the table, dish by dish, never more than one at a time. While the guests were busy eating one dish, the architricline cut up and served out another into portions that would then be presented: this way of serving a large meal is convenient and uncomplicated. After the soup, almost all the dishes were beautiful sea fish . . . I was there as a spectator, among a great crowd of onlookers.[26]

While the learned President gazed in wonderment (even the practicality of the table service could impress a Frenchman accustomed to a different order of courses), beneath his eyes there unfolded this astonishing violet-coloured scene dominated by the cassock-wearing architricline, by the cœnobite abbot of the holy Vatican feasts. In the meantime the vicar-cardinal, 'a good monk,

THE LAVISH TABLE 147

Carmelite bigot, genuine Sulpician', waited devoutly to 'devour in all humility a sturgeon and to drink like a templar'.[27]

It was then that a member of the Holy College, Cardinal de Tencin, turning to the vicar (the Carmelite Guadagni) and stealing a sly glance at his pale face, whispered to him 'in a tender and smarmy tone of voice': 'Your Eminence is none too well and, methinks, is not eating.'

The noble Burgundian-cum-Savoyard Charles de Brosses, a great admirer of Sallust and of the ancient ruins of Herculaneum, commonly regarded as a man 'of unprecedented and superlative greediness',[28] was also a friend of Cardinal Lambertini and of the very erudite Passionei, the chief librarian at the Vatican Library. De Brosses was a renowned collector of manuscripts and books and was well known not only for his remarkable freedom of both thought and expression but also for his devotion to good food ('a daily entertainment that constitutes one of society's principal bonds').[29] This French noble was therefore a perspicacious observer not only of 'antiquities' but also of Italian culinary customs. In Rome he was so deeply affected by a pudding that was served to him by the keeper of the Mont d'Or inn that, having seized the recipe and left the establishment, he ran straight to another cook who prepared it for him 'in an astonishing way'.

> It is something, my friend, that far surpasses the cream tarts of Bedreddin-Hassan, which elicit such pathetic and theatrical acknowledgement in the *Thousand and One Nights*.[30]

As a good antiquarian and lapidary, De Brosses decided to preserve the recipe of this dream-sweet, capable of conjuring up cream fantasies worthy of the *Thousand and One Nights*, and whose oriental flavours opened up new perspectives for the learned President's imagination.

> Take plenty of beef marrow, and even more breadcrumbs soaked in milk, almond paste, cinnamon and currants, mix together in a mass, as with bread, and stew in a pan full of excellent stock, covered by a fine cloth. Then cook for a second time in a pie dish so that it forms a crust. Eat a lot of this if you have a strong stomach, in other

words, eat as much as that glutton Sainte-Palaye, and declare that Martialot is nothing but a pompous fool for failing to give this recipe pride of place in his *Cuisinier français*. I would only argue that there are too many currants in it.'[31]

At Rome, in contrast to the game which he considered only mediocre, De Brosses particularly appreciated 'ordinary things', which he thought very good indeed: 'bread, fruit, large meats, especially beef, which I cannot praise highly enough, and which you will judge when I have told you that it outstrips Paris beef as much as Paris beef outstrips that of small provincial towns'.[32] As for Italian fruit, the erudite Frenchman was rather disappointed.

> It is true to say that fruit is more varied and mostly of better quality in France than in Italy, apart from grapes, figs and melons, three excellent species that are better here than among us. Bologna grapes are without compare. It is possible to find in Paris both figs and melons that are as tasty as the ones here: but here this kind of fruit is perfectly common and commonly perfect. Last autumn, in Italy, I ate no plums or peaches at all that were as good as ours.[33]

But the Tiber sturgeon that he had tasted at the residence of Cardinal Acquaviva of Aragona, certainly the wealthiest prelate in Rome and a man who loved 'pleasure, women and good victuals', seemed to him to be worthy of Apicius. Being an excellent connoisseur, as much of slitheringly fresh sea flesh as of old parchments, the quick-witted De Brosses opined that the sturgeon was 'of an exquisite taste, quite unlike the ordinary run of Mediterranean fish, which are worth far less than those from the Ocean'.[34]

In Italy this perfect connoisseur of the 'science of *savoir vivre*' did not note the absence of 'certain social delicacies' which, according to Pietro Verri, were the exclusive property of the French, quite unknown to Italians and especially to those of 'the southern part'[35] of the long and many centred peninsula. During one of his long stays in Rome, spanning the end of Clement XII's papacy and the beginning of that of Benedict XIV (who, during conclave, was known to whisper to the cardinals 'in his saucy and bantering tone:

"if you want a fine dolt, take me"'),[36] De Brosses expressed an opinion in direct opposition to that of the Milanese illuminist Verri. Comparing the 'different forms that magnificence assumes in the two nations', the Burgundian found that Italian liberality was 'infinitely more rich, more noble, more agreeable, more useful, more magnificent, and more conscious of its own air of grandeur'.[37] In particular, he carefully examined the French craving to 'cut a fine figure' and to 'have a fine house', which was mainly confined to convivial ceremonial, and to the determination to 'keep a fine table', noting also that costly and sumptuous gastronomy was the only passport to high society. De Brosses finally reached the conclusion that the exclusively Italian passion for architectural magnificence in its villas and palaces was much wiser than the pomp and ceremony of French banquets, inasmuch as it was more intelligent to 'feast one's eyes than to feast one's palate'.

'Gallic spirit' and, indeed, the 'hoggishness' of Italy's transalpine neighbours could easily lead to the squandering of resources and to the questionable superiority of the French in 'the professions of luxury'.[38] A devotion to architectural splendour, on the other hand, by promoting 'the professions of essential need', might entrust to posterity the memory and glory of its noble forefathers. In France, in contrast to the measured and 'frugal life' of Italians,

> a rich man who entertains has to have many cooks, many entrée and sweet services, many elegant fruit services (the use of which, incidentally, we have adopted from the Italians). There must always be three times as much profusion of dishes as the number of guests would require. Such a man gathers together the greatest possible number of people to consume the dainties prepared, without worrying too much whether or not the people invited are pleasant. What matters is that people should see that he supplies the most exquisite and best-served food anywhere and that the word should go forth that nobody knows better than he how to do honour to his wealth. In the midst of all this expense, he lives in difficulties from day to day, without pleasure, even with some real trouble: uneasy despite his great wealth; often ruined, and certainly quite forgotten the instant his guests have digested his food.[39]

Given that these lines were written by the 'superlatively' greedy De Brosses, they have about them a ring of personal confession: the dutiful self-flagellation of a quasi-repentant glutton who in order to secure a reduction in his sentence would go so far as to exclaim: 'a fine-fluted column is just as appreciable as a fine hazel-grouse'.[40] For such a Pantagruelist as the learned President,[41] this must have involved considerable and painful sacrifice. His opinion on the frugality of the Italians was not new. The 'sinewy and shivery Francesco Redi', known also as the 'mummy', had referred to Italy's 'customary parsimony' as it contrasted to France, 'where all men are quick spirited, bright, witty and vivacious', 'accustomed naturally to feeding themselves with a broader hand'. Redi attributed this characteristic to the French climate and to the French people's natural ethnic bent: 'the peoples of France are generally very great eaters'.

An expert on purges and enemas and a theoretician of dainty diets and mild therapies, Redi was wary of 'great and famous doctors' and downright scornful of the 'mysterious' recipes that apothecaries touted, 'vile concoctions that used an infinity of herbs from a hundred different dioceses, with all those names beginning "hiero-", and those blessed laxative plants, those diacattoliconum and those diafiniconum', bristling with 'those impossible, deafening and wiseacre names' ('Lithontripticinum the electuary, / And Diatriontonpiperycinum'). As a cool-headed naturalist, he preferred to rely on nature and on fresh waters. Indeed, in his dithyrambic poem 'Arianna inferma' Bacchus' wife is devoured by fever as a result of her eagerness to imitate her husband's excesses. Yet Redi understood and was ready to excuse French intemperance 'because it is due not to gluttony but to nature and this particular nature is not at all modern but, on the contrary, very ancient. After all, Sulpicius Severus, in his *Dialogo delle virtù de' monaci orientali*, stated quite clearly: *Voracitas in Graecia gula est, in Gallis natura* [Voracity is due to gluttony in Greece but to nature in France].'[42] Since it belonged to the realm of nature, the staggering appetite of the French was not to be classed as a vice but rather as a kind of natural cupidity that had been programmed by the all-knowing Mother. President de Brosses, who was unlikely to have been familiar with Redi and his opinions, took the view that

> the Italians are not so mistaken when they poke fun, in their turn, at our kind of ostentation, commenting that *tutto se ne va al cacatoio* (their own comical expression) and arguing that it is no more unreasonable for them to accuse our great nobles of baseness because they build no public buildings than for us to reproach them for not providing anything to eat.[43]

It is a strange point of view, almost paradoxical, detached from reality. Above all it fails to take account of the differences between the two types of civilization, the one architectural, the other literary. Pier Iacopo Martello, who was very familiar with French customs and *civilisation*, had analysed in the 'proceedings' of 'Il vero parigino italiano' the distinctive features of each country's culture, entering into a polemic with a French abbot who was

> eager to prove to me that the best taste, both in poetic art and in oratory, had gone to the other side of the mountains, to his darling France, among the fabrics and the wigs, in the barouche and coupé carriages, under the head-dresses in whose manufacture France surpasses any other kingdom.[44]

The great aristocratic palaces that President de Brosses so admired, their 'endless suites of rooms', struck Martello's 'Parisian' interlocutor as a pointless display of grandeur. In his view they were luxurious but uncomfortable sanctuaries of magnificence, where in exchange 'for the pleasure of enjoying paintings, tapestries, tableware and statues'

> you die of cold in the winter, unless you wrap yourself up in carpets; and you die of heat in the summer, unless you throw off even the sheets to uncover your soaking and naked body. There is such an excess of air, either freezing or scorching, to which the weather outside communicates its intemperance via the large windows that are never quite closed and the many broad doors that

> breathe through their locks and cracks, tormenting your wretched body with shivers or with fevers. In the morning they rise, punished, as it were, for their mad taste for magnificence. These palaces, huge machines of which there are plenty in Rome, more than in any other metropolis, contain one or more sumptuous apartments that are only used for certain functions for a few hours a year. The rest of the time they are inhabited by flies, mosquitoes, spiders and mice, which, if they could be satisfied by opulent decorations, would be enormously proud to romp around among the brocades, velvets, damasks, gold and silver, laughing to scorn such crazed proprietors, panting their way to the top of these piles, and then settling down to dwell and rest in a few cramped rooms.[45]

These gold-decorated and very imposing but equally uncomfortable palaces-cum-museums were nowhere less functional than in the 'arrangement of the kitchens',

> from where, in order to reach the place where the gentleman takes his lunch or dinner, dishes have to embark upon a journey lasting a quarter of an hour, entrusted into the hands of servants who, unless they are complete dolts, are sure to have a quick taste along the way. The food therefore arrives cold and unattractive. Otherwise, to keep it warm, the food has to be brought with so much heat that, when they are placed on the tables, to prevent stomachs from growing cold, the heads of the banqueters are inflamed.[46]

Unlike Italians, the 'modern French', who 'are fond of comfortable architecture', in their 'private dwellings', were closer to the ancient Romans and to their practical sense of the functional. The houses not just of great lords but of modest tradespeople were a model of elegant and simple architecture. There was nothing in Italy that could compare with the delights of French *cabinets*.

> But you, what do you think of those *cabinets*, my dear Martello? Is it possible to imagine any human thing more delicate and charming than a French *cabinet*? The little pictures, the *buccheri*, the porcelains and the mirrors that from all sides multiply the beautiful and harmoniously arranged little objects, creating an atmosphere of luxury and elegance. And those little libraries so well divided into

compartments, with their painted and gold-decorated shelves, all lined with little furbelows which, running from end to end, decorate and equalize the appearance of the books and preserve them from dust! Do not the spacious table and writing-desk, the furbished steel letter-press, the seals, the paper, the quills, which, neatly aligned, do not encumber but rather adorn the desk, invite and impel one, though gently, to find recreation in studying? And, at the same time, in the view of whoever sits at the desk, are not the sun by day and the lamp by night multiplied a hundred times over by as many dazzling mirrors, set in recesses and variously arranged overhead and to the sides?[47]

A French dining-room, quiet, warm, comfortable and 'of a height that neither overheats nor chills the heads of the diners and is roomy enough to allow people to move around', was very different from one of those splendid but uninhabitable rooms in Italian, and especially Roman, palaces, be they of the 'Farnese, Barberini, Borghese or Panfili' variety. Built on a human scale, rather than on one fit for demigods or heroes, French dining-rooms offered that simple comfort with which Pier Iacopo Martello was familiar:

> being in one such room, you will meet a mask of white marble, pouring water into glasses. In the corners of the same room you will see painted and inlaid buffet shelves: here you encounter a round table, neither excessively high, nor particularly low, and with a circumference well suited to the needs of a family. Lastly, chairs arranged in a circle, easy to shift, comfortable and light rather than opulent.[48]

A few decades later, in 1762, another noble, cosmopolitan and learned Bolognese physician, Giovanni Lodovico Bianconi, in a letter that he sent from Dresden to the young marquis Filippo Ercolani, again emphasized the profound differences separating the French pleasure and joy in the ephemeral and, on the other hand, Roman eternity. Bianconi, a sophisticated art connoisseur and protector of the young Winckelmann, was willing, however, to acknowledge the numerous novelties that the 'delicacy of [Gallic] good taste' had introduced into house interiors and gardens.

France has always been inclined towards things that are joyful and short-lived, so it is not surprising that Roman majesty and civil architecture have made so little progress in France while the interior decoration of houses and the elegance of pergolas, greenery and fountains have made so much. I should like you to see the garden of the Marquise de Pompadour, designed and planted at Bellevue; there you see in miniature just how far the beauty of nature and the delicacy of good taste can go. Among other delights, there is a little wood consisting entirely of multicoloured roses climbing up iron stakes that support them but that they cover and hide. I do not know if anything could be more delicious or more pleasant to behold. As you meander through this beautiful copse, you lose yourself in a cloud of heavenly and reinvigorating scents; and, surely, the sacred avenues of Gnidus and Paestum could hardly have been more charming or sweeter smelling than these. In the middle, more exactly, at the top of a green hill, stands an excellently built little palace, all decorated with fine marble, bronzes, busts, vases, porcelains and the finest carpets from Siam and China. From there you can see, only four miles from Italy, the immense city of Paris with its towering buildings and, stretching beneath you, the Seine as it winds its way across a huge and blossoming plain. Just imagine for yourselves what the French say of our albeit magnificent societies when, full of these ideas, they arrive in Rome. We can show off the beauty of the statues of Polygnotus or the bas-reliefs of Athenodorus and display the urns and other rarities of Villa Albani or of Pinciana: but it is not enough to please them. Yet whatever they say, today they would have neither Marly nor Versailles if they had not formerly seen the villas of Tivoli or of Frascati; even if now, like an old and greying matron, they show the wrinkles of old age, and are clothed in the fashion of Leo X or of Pope Julius.[49]

Considered from the viewpoint of 'things that are joyful and short-lived', fleeting and shifting pleasures, delights and spells that are soon obsolete, the French taste for intimacy, and hence for delicacy, achieved its highest perfection in rococo style. Nothing could appear more seductive than 'a tiny and out of the way room in a lonely place',[50] nothing could be more conducive of 'solitude' and 'abandonment' than a discreet and hidden 'hermitage'. The miniaturization of the countryside and the shrinking of physical objects lead to an interiorization of pleasure. The eye has to be treated to pleasing objects, of just the right size but tending towards well-tempered gracefulness, whether it is a 'small palace' or a 'pavilion' or a hothouse that contains and manages within its controlled indoor environment exotic plant worlds that came into being under the banner of disorder and amidst the primordial chaos of the forest, 'foreign wonders', rare essences now domesticated and catalogued. Like food, every different object has to be 'approved by taste' and, at the same time, must 'be charming to our eyes'.[51] Such are the demands of 'fresh youth' and 'brilliant gaiety', such are the dictates of the sophisticated principles of 'modern luxury', in submission to the pleasures of the eye, to chromatic voluptuousness. Surveying a range of fowl, one's eyes would be magnetically drawn to 'show birds',[52] to the 'crimson gold of the pheasant', to the 'spangled guinea-fowl'. Their strange beauty would appear to act almost as a stimulus to taste. Enough to make one suppose that eyes could be the antennae of internal pleasure, visual tasters connected to the hidden caverns of the viscera.

Jacques Delille, a landscape planner, a man devoted to the mathematical organization of fields and gardens, was enchanted by hothouses where, sheltering them from any inclemency and by violating the logic of the seasons, 'fruits of a false summer' and 'flowers of a false spring'[53] could be made respectively to ripen and to blossom in fake weather detached from the secret rhythms of nature.

> But I love to see these roofs, these see-through shelters
> Receiving from different climates a variety of tribute,
> This haven where Iberian jasmine grows hardy,
> Where the cold-loathing periwinkle forgets its home
> And the yellow pineapple, fooled by the heat,
> Yields the extorted treasure of its fruit.[54]

Never would Abbot Roberti, who (like Giuseppe Baretti) adored the *charcuterie* of 'our own ingenious grocers', have turned down San Michele ham or a shoulder of San Secondo in favour of ham from Bayonne. And, in his view, mortadella from Bologna was unrivalled.

> Several years ago, at a meeting with certain Bologna professors, I raised that great question: was it possible, of an evening, without violating the laws of healthy living, to eat several slices of mortadella? They replied in great seriousness, extremely learned as they were, that pork meat was quite possibly more healthy than beef.[55]

It is not known whether Count Pietro Verri, who shared Piero Iacopo Martello's love of chocolate, that 'delicious and beneficial beverage',[56] included pork under his heading of 'heavy and viscous meats'; but there is no doubt that the Bolognese response to sensualist cuisine was not the one he would have expected. Even when he was in Paris, Martello would not pass up the opportunity of 'gulping down a plate of macaroni with butter and cheese from Italy, at the liberal, straightforward and Lombard table'[57] of the erudite Count Pighetti, ambassador of the Duchy of Parma to the French court. Bologna, the Etruscans' ancient Felsina, distrusted – and not only on literary grounds – 'us French' who were so determined to 'maintain the order and the arrangement of dishes, from their fragrant soups right through to their towering desserts'.[58] They were as faithful to the immutable maintenance of syntactic order in the succession of dishes brought to table as they were naturally hostile in their prose to the 'perturbation of grammatical order'.[59]

Bologna was a city with a talent for mediation and, even at this tricky juncture in the development of taste, somehow managed with even-handedness to pursue the art of carefully balancing old and new. The city's 'sumptuous' cuisine, of prelatic and senatorial tradition, leaning towards conservatism, was perhaps not quite able to compete with the refinements of the eighteenth-century Piedmontese 'buffet' ('for us, a court of arbitration on many questions of elegance'),[60] nor with culinary achievements of the Bourbon courts of Parma or of Naples. Count Benvenuto Robbio di San Rafaele, a member of the Accademia dei Filopatridi and a poet of the pre-Risorgimento who had written a 'little poem' in free verse entitled 'L'Italia' (1772), courteously reproached Abbot Roberti for his excessive love of ham, which he thought 'a nasty meat, salted and smoked'.[61] Count Benvenuto, who was a gentleman of the chamber of Vittorio Amedeo III, accordingly invited the Abbot to try out some delicacies of a quite different order, to immerse himself in a sea of chocolate, little biscuits, sweetmeats, cakes, to plunge to the bottom of a deep dark lake, perfumed by white foaming sugar, in the hot whirlpool of Piedmontese dainties.

> I should like to send you a cauldron full of a thick and well-whipped chocolate, made with genuine Soconosco cocoa and enlivened with the most mischievous of vanilla with, floating on the surface, a felucca woven with little Vercelli buns, paved with biscuits from Novara or Chieri, its sides encrusted with mosaics made with sweets from Mondovì. In the middle there would be a small temple built with ring-shaped cakes, sugar-coated sweets flavoured with citron, peach, quince, and many other tasty dainties that the innocent hands of our nuns spend their time producing during their brief moments of idleness. By way of a globe, the dome of the little temple would have one of those masterpieces of confectionery that come from the monasteries of Asti; and all around, in perfect order, there would be a variety of statues representing Phoebus, the Muses and the poetic horse, too often mounted by too many knights; and the said statues would be made not of glass or of porcelain but of superfine dazzling-white sugar.[62]

Dazzling-white sugar, ground down from huge Dutch sugar loaves, 'hard, white, shiny, stony, crunchy, light',[63] sweeter and more yielding than Venetian sugar loaves, the white gold of confectioners and pastry-cooks. *Le siècle de la femme* was crazy about chocolate, which it celebrated in both prose and verse, and worshipped sugar, which was now finding its way into everything. Under the skilful hands of pastry-cook architects, sugar caught people's eye and slipped down their throats, in rosolios, syrups, sorbets, jellies, conserves, candied fruits and flowers, in undulating wreaths of 'such pretty-looking' icing sugar, and in multicoloured dessert decoration.

A velvety, sugary fever penetrated patrician palaces and Jesuitical homes alike. The epic of chocolate and sugar had found its most devoted worshippers and most fervent eulogists among the descendants of St Ignatius.

> Oh sweetness, oh sugar, oh dearest gift
> Delivered to us from foreign lands!
> Death to anyone, mean or stupid,
> Who would prize you less, oh vital sugar!
> Death to whoever would play the sad game
> Of offering a person tart Turkish coffee:
> Death to whoever would daringly venture
> To make, without you, either pastilles or tarts.
>
> Though weary, hoarse and rusty
> By taking you, one's voice grows clear;
> The tender peach and bitter walnut
> Are both by you candied and coated
> So hostile winter can do no harm
> By making their flesh too tough or soft:
> And the green pistachio, befriended by you,
> Is turned into white and immortal candy.
>
> From Virginia and from Caracas,
> The Moluccas and far Macao,
> Others wait for cinnamon,
> Vanilla, cocoa and carnations;
> And that which modern noses yearn,
> Like Helen searching for Menelaus,
> Powder from Brazil and Havana,
> Soft, subtle and sweetly scented.
>
> And so shall I pray to Father Neptune,
> Often to dispatch sugared goods towards
> Janus' daughter, from Adria to her mother,
> With courtesy and safe from all offence;
> And, that they reach fine Italian shores
> Quickly, strike them with your trident!

Those nuns who love to make sweet ring-cakes
In my own presence express such wishes.[64]

But by the first decade of the nineteenth century this gentle art of using powder as building material and embalming the ephemeral was already suffering the bitterest of death throes. The *douceur de vivre* had been buried by the downfall of the old regime, society had changed, taste moved on. Arabesqued landscapes, delicate classically inspired perspectives and airy sugar-built feats of architecture were going out of fashion. Noble eyes would no longer pause at a floral paradise frozen in sweetish dough, nor linger over frosted emblems or candied allegories and would merely glide absent-mindedly over any artificial gardens that happened to bloom in the midst of sugar. This form of art was burning itself out: the days of sugar's elegant epic were numbered. When in 1807 he announced the unstoppable decline of spun pastilles, Francesco Leonardi, an artist who had survived the ruin of the old world, recited a funeral oration to the art of the buffet.

Only a few years ago tables were still laid with grand magnificence. The decoration of the dessert, the most beautiful and most striking feature, usually echoed the theme evoked by the most colourful and sophisticated of the tables. In Italy we have had outstanding artists who were not only highly skilled in the fields of confectionery, biscuit-baking, sorbets, ice-creams and so on but who brought, moreover, many other special talents, immense genius and a fertile imagination to the creation of the most beautiful *works of decoration*, some of which represented the greatest actions of distinguished men or remarkable events from the history of nations. Temples, groups, ornaments, coats of arms, balustrades, vases, figures, etc.: nothing that the very best drawing, architecture and good taste could contribute to such efforts was neglected. Parterres, moreover, formed the most graceful of arabesques in the most beautiful or most lively of colours; and natural flowers were arranged with art and a sense of symmetry to make the *dessert* a joy to behold.

These elegant and sumptuous pieces of work were all created using nothing but pastille paste; the *parterre sablé*, for its part, was made using the very finest sands in a variety of colours and shades.

[Coloured sands have been used in the last few years, but – commented F. Leonardi – it was not long ago that Dutch sugar loaves were used for 'sanding' the dessert in various colours. This method, however, was not perfect, since flies not only rapidly damaged the most beautiful and elegant of drawing work, but they also upset the banqueters. This is how the idea arose of replacing sugar with something else that would have the same function, and it was found that calcined and finely pulverized marble would act as a perfect stand-in.][65]

Now, I do not know quite for what reason, but today all of this has changed, perhaps because people, always willing to accommodate alterations in questions of taste, believed that a more straightforward service was more appropriate to their philosophical system. The dessert is now composed of nothing but a very few *plateaux* covered with mirrors, a few porcelain groups and figurines, some flower vases, and that is all . . .

I hope, however, that one day, when the Temple of Janus has been closed and wealthy men begin again to enjoy the delights of the table, not only will past dainties reappear on magnificent tables, but good taste, delicacy, ornamentation and sumptuousness will be carried further in such a domain that shapes the pleasures of society and distracts men for a while from the hazards of their lives.[66]

The great artist of the buffet was deceived. When the Temple of Janus was in fact briefly closed, at the end of the scorching Napoleonic period, any return to the pomp and magnificence of the *ancien régime* remained but a dream entertained only by aged artists and nostalgic aristocrats. 'Good taste', drawing, architecture: the 'lively and joyful imagination' of eighteenth-century society was reborn neither on Restoration tables nor in the dull cuisine of the Romantic period. The fabulous 1780s faded and were forgotten: the age of sugar and of confectionery masterpieces was buried for ever.

NOTES

CHAPTER 1 THE SCIENCE OF *SAVOIR VIVRE*

1 *Carteggio di Pietro e di Alessandro Verri dal 1766 al 1797*, vol. vi, ed. E. Greppi and A. Giulini (Milan, Cogliati, 1928), p. 1.
2 Giuseppe Parini, 'Il Mezzogiorno', lines 205ff.
3 Ibid., lines 209–24.
4 Francesco Algarotti, 'Lettere varie', pt i, in *Opere del conte Algarotti edizione novissima* (Venice, Carlo Palese, 1792), vol. ix, pp. 236–7.
5 Saverio Bettinelli, *Dialoghi d'Amore*, pt ii, in *Opere edite e inedite in prosa ed in versi dell'abate Saverio Bettinelli*, 2nd edn (Venice, Adolfo Cesare, 1799), vol. vi, p. 165.
6 Ibid., p. 166.
7 Algarotti, 'Lettere varie', in *Opere*, vol. ix, p. 19.
8 Ibid., p. 142.
9 Bettinelli, *Dialoghi d'Amore*, p. 166.
10 Ibid.
11 Ibid., pp. 166–7.
12 Ibid., p. 167.
13 Ibid., p. 169.
14 Ibid., p. 168.
15 Ibid.
16 Ibid., pp. 168–9.
17 Ibid., p. 169.
18 Parini, 'Il Mezzogiorno', lines 383–6.
19 Algarotti, 'Lettere varie', p. 19.
20 Ibid., p. 18.

21 Ibid., p. 17.
22 Francesco Algarotti, 'Pensieri diversi', in *Opere*, vol. vii, p. 57.
23 Ferdinando Galiani, *Dialogo sulle donne e altri scritti*, ed. C. Cases (Milan, Feltrinelli, 1957), p. 27.
24 Algarotti, 'Lettere varie', p. 187.
25 Ibid., p. 164.
26 Saverio Bettinelli, 'Lettere a Lesbia Cidonia sopra gli epigrammi', in *Opere edite e inedite*, vol. xxi, p. 32.
27 Ibid., p. 25.
28 Ibid., p. 39.
29 Ibid., p. 40.
30 Ibid.
31 Ibid., p. 40.
32 Algarotti, 'Lettere varie', p. 163.
33 Bettinelli, 'Lettere a Lesbia Cidonia', p. 41.
34 Ibid., p. 40.
35 'La Cauchoise ou Mémoires d'une courtisane célèbre', in *Œuvres anonymes du XVIIIe siècle* (Fayard, 1985), Enfer de la Bibliothèque nationale, vol. iii, p. 420.
36 François de Sade, *Les 120 journées de Sodome ou l'École du libertinage* (UGE, 1975), vol. i, p. 134.
37 Jean-Baptiste Drouet de Maupertuy, *Les avantures d'Euphormion, histoire satyrique* (Amsterdam, Janssons à Waesberge, 1712), vol. ii, pp. 8–9. This is the eighteenth-century French version of a work with the same title by the Scotsman John Barclay, published in 1605.
38 De Maupertuy, *Les avantures*, p. 10.

CHAPTER 2 THE REVENGE OF THE NIGHT

1 Charles-Louis de Montesquieu, *Cahiers, 1716–1755*, ed. Bernard Grasset (Paris, Grasset, 1941), p. 243.
2 Pietro Verri, 'Discorso sull'indole del piacere e del dolore', in *Del piacere e del dolore ed altri scritti di filosofia ed economia*, ed. R. De Felice (Milan, Feltrinelli, 1964), p. 44.
3 *Encyclopédie ou dictionnaire raisonné des sciences, des arts et des métiers*, vol. iii, p. 762.
4 *Ricordi overo ammaestramenti di Monsig. Sabba Castiglione cavaliere gerosolimitano* (Venice, Michele Bonelli, 1574), fol. 25r.; 1st edn (Venice, 1554).

5 Cristoforo Muzani, 'Costume di vivere inutile e ozioso', in *Quaresimale di celebri moderni autori italiani*, 2nd edn (Venice, Tipografia Curti, 1822), vol. i, p. 155.
6 Ibid., p. 167.
7 Giovanni Piva, 'Carattere del secolo XVIII', in *Quaresimale*, vol. ii, p. 68.
8 Muzani, 'Costume', p. 164.
9 Antonino Valsecchi, O.P., 'Spiriti forti del secolo', in *Quaresimale*, vol. i, p. 137.
10 Ibid., p. 138.
11 Ibid., p. 147.
12 Ibid., p. 136.
13 Ibid., p. 143.
14 Ibid., p. 145.
15 Ibid., p. 146.
16 Muzani, 'Costume', pp. 161–2.
17 Ibid., p. 163.
18 Ibid.
19 Ergasto Acrivio, 'Le notti alla moda', in *Satirette morali e piacevoli* (Foligno, Tomassini Stamperia, 1794), p. 71. Ergasto Acrivio was a pseudonym used by the Capuchin friar Francesco Maria da Bologna.
20 Ibid., p. 74.
21 Ibid.
22 Giovambatista Roberti, 'Lusso', in *Quaresimale*, vol. iii, p. 153.
23 Pier Luigi Grossi, 'Dei peccati del secolo XVIII', in *Quaresimale*, vol. i, pp. 94–6.
24 Piva, 'Carattere', p. 67.
25 Grossi, 'Dei peccati', p. 95. The quotations that follow are taken from the same sermon.
26 Francesco Franceschini, 'Libero vestire delle donne', in *Quaresimale*, vol. iv, p. 168.
27 Grossi, 'Dei peccati', p. 95. The quotations that follow are taken from the same sermon.
28 Pier Maria da Pederoba, 'Fine dell'uomo', in *Quaresimale*, vol. ii, p. 196.
29 Vincenzo Giorgi, 'Matrimonio', in *Quaresimale*, vol. iv, p. 90.
30 Ibid., p. 89.
31 Ibid., p. 90.
32 Saverio Bettinelli, *Dialoghi d'Amore*, in *Opere edite e inedite in prosa ed in versi dell'abate Saverio Bettinelli*, 2nd edn (Venice, Adolfo Cesare,

1799), vol. vi, p. 170.
33 Ibid., pp. 170–1.
34 Ibid., p. 169.
35 *La Toletta* (Bologna, 1788), p. xix. The lines are by Abbot Clementino Vannetti.
36 Grossi, 'Dei peccati', p. 104.
37 Ibid.
38 Francesco Algarotti, 'Epistole in versi', in *Opere del conte Algarotti edizione novissima* (Venice, Carlo Palese, 1792), vol. i, p. 59: 'A S.E. il Signor Alessandro Zeno Procuratore di s. Marco. Sopra il commercio'.
39 Algarotti, 'Epistole in versi', p. 20: 'A Fillide'.
40 Lorenzo Magalotti, *Lettere familiari del conte Lorenzo Magalotti e di altri insigni uomini a lui scritte* (Florence, Cambiagi, 1769), pt ii, p. 190.
41 Algarotti, 'Epistole in versi', pp. 19–20: 'A Fillide'.
42 Antonmaria Perotti, 'Gli imenei festeggiati nella deliziosa, e magnificentissima villa detta il Castellazzo', in *Rime per le felicissime nozze del Signor Conte Don Galeazzo Arconati Visconti colla Signora Contessa Donna Innocenzia Casati* (Milan, Francesco Agnelli, 1744), p. 124. Perotti (a Carmelite friar who belonged to the congregation of Mantua) was known to the Arcadians as Egimo Afroditico. The brief quotation on 'noble thirsts' is taken from the same epithalamium, p. 126.
43 Adeodato Turchi, 'Omelia intorno all'influenza delle vesti su la morale cristiana. Diretta al suo popolo nel giorno di Tutt'i Santi l'anno 1800', in *Nova raccolta delle omelie e indulti di Adeodato Turchi* (Parma, 1800; Rimini, G. Marsoner, 1800), p. 17.
44 Francesco Albergati Capacelli, *Lettere capricciose di Francesco Albergati Capacelli e di Francesco Zacchiroli dai medesimi capricciosamente stampate*, in *Opere drammatiche complete e scelte prose di Francesco Albergati Capacelli* (Bologna, Emidio Dall'Olmo, 1827), p. 303. The first edition of the *Lettere capricciose* was published in Venice in 1780 (Pasquali). The note in square brackets is by Albergati.
45 Grossi, 'Dei peccati', p. 97.
46 Ibid.
47 Ibid., p. 102.
48 Francesco Algarotti, 'Pensieri diversi', in *Opere*, vol. vii, p. 57.
49 Adeodato Turchi, *Omelia . . . recitata nel giorno di Tutt'i Santi dell'anno 1794 sopra l'amore di novità* (Rimini, G. Marsoner, n.d.), p. 8.

50 Ibid.
51 Ibid., pp. 9–10.
52 Roberti, 'Lusso', p. 156. The quotations that follow are from the same sermon.
53 Ibid., p. 155.
54 Ibid., p. 153.
55 Grossi, 'Dei peccati', p. 97.
56 Ergasto Acrivio, 'Le villeggiature', in *Satirette morali e piacevoli*, pp. 37–9.

CHAPTER 3 GOOD COOKS AND SKILFUL HAIRDRESSERS

1 Giovambatista Roberti, 'Lettera sopra il canto de' pesci', in *Raccolta di varie operette del padre Giovambatista Roberti della Compagnia di Gesù* (Bologna, Lelio dalla Volpe, 1767), vol. ii, p. xiii.
2 Quoted in De Cussy, 'L'art culinaire', in *Les classiques de la table à l'usage des praticiens et des gens du monde* (Paris, Martinon, 1844), p. 263.
3 Ibid.
4 Ibid., p. 257.
5 Ibid.
6 Ibid.
7 Marie-Antoinin Carême, 'Aphorismes, pensées et maximes', in *Les classiques de la table*, p. 363.
8 Ibid.
9 Quoted in De Cussy, 'L'art culinaire', p. 263.
10 Ibid., p. 257.
11 Ibid.
12 Ibid., pp. 257–8.
13 Charles-Louis de Montesquieu, *Cahiers, 1716–1755*, ed. Bernard Grasset (Paris, Grasset, 1941), p. 236.
14 Ibid., p. 189.
15 Ibid., p. 190.
16 De Cussy, 'L'art culinaire', p. 287.
17 Montesquieu, *Cahiers*, p. 166.
18 Ibid., p. 190.
19 Giovambatista Roberti, 'Ad un Professore di Belle Lettere nel Friuli', in *Raccolta di varie operette dell'Abate Conte Giovambatista Roberti* (Bologna, Lelio dalla Volpe, 1785), vol. iv, pp. vi–vii.

20 Giovambatista Roberti, 'Risposta del padre Giovambatista Roberti al Conte di S. Rafaele', in *Scelta di lettere erudite del padre Giovambatista Roberti* (Venice, Tipografia di Alvisopoli, 1825), p. 217.
21 Giovambatista Roberti, 'Lettera a sua Eccellenza Pietro Zaguri sopra la semplicità elegante', in *Raccolta di operette dell'Abate Conte*, vol. iv, pp. i–xviii.
22 See Giovambatista Roberti, 'Lettera ad un vecchio e ricco Signore feudatario sopra il lusso del secolo XVIII', in *Scelta di lettere erudite*, pp. 119–49.
23 Ibid., p. 121.

CHAPTER 4 THE PURGED CENTURY

1 Francesco Algarotti, 'Pensieri diversi', in *Opere del conte Algarotti edizione novissima* (Venice, Carlo Palese, 1792), vol. vii, p. 148.
2 Giovambatista Roberti, 'Lettera ad un vecchio e ricco Signore feudatario sopra il lusso del secolo XVIII', in *Scelta di lettere erudite del padre Giovambatista Roberti* (Venice, Tipografia di Alvisopoli, 1825), pp. 124–6.
3 See Peter Burke, 'Conspicuous Consumption in Seventeenth-century Italy' (1982); repr. in *Historical Anthropology of Early Modern Italy* (Cambridge University Press, 1987), pp. 132–49.
4 Roberti, 'Lettera ad un vecchio e ricco Signore feudatario', p. 120.
5 Charles de Saint-Evremond, *Œuvres meslées* (London, Jacob Tonson, 1705), vol. ii, p. 462.
6 Ibid.
7 Ibid., p. 464.
8 Ibid., p. 551.
9 Ibid., p. 550.
10 Ibid., p. 551.
11 Lorenzo Magalotti, *Lettere familiari* [against atheism] (Venice, S. Coleti, 1732), pt i, p. 202. On the 'Corsican oysters', see the letter from Francesco Redi to Valerio Inghirami of 30 March 1667.
12 Saint-Evremond, *Œuvres meslées*, vol. ii, p. 551.
13 Ibid., p. 462.
14 Lorenzo Magalotti, *Lettere sopra i buccheri con l'aggiunta di lettere contro l'ateismo, scientifiche e erudite e di relazioni varie*, ed. M. Praz (Florence, Le Monnier, 1945), p. 72.
15 Ibid., pp. 90–1.

16 This poem is included in 'Annotazioni di Francesco Redi al Ditirambo', in *Opere di Francesco Redi* (Milan, Società tipografica de' classici italiani, 1809), vol. i, p. 293.
17 Lorenzo Magalotti, 'Il Contento. Vivanda inglese', in *Canzonette anacreontiche di Lindoro Elateo Pastore Arcade* (Florence, Tartini and Franchi, 1723), pp. 73-6.
18 Ibid., p. 72. The fundamental text remains A. Graf, *L'anglomania e l'influsso inglese in Italia nel secolo XVIII* (Turin, Loescher, 1911); on Magalotti, see pp. 243, 406-7 and *passim*.
19 Lorenzo Magalotti, *Lettere del Conte Lorenzo Magalotti Gentiluomo fiorentino* (Florence, Giuseppe Manni, 1736), p. 77.
20 Lorenzo Magalotti, 'Diario di Francia dell'anno 1668', in *Relazioni di viaggio in Inghilterra Francia e Svezia*, ed. W. Moretti (Bari, Laterza, 1968), pp. 212-13.
21 Magalotti, *Lettere sopra i buccheri*, p. 310.

CHAPTER 5 HEAVY AND VISCOUS MEATS

1 Francesco Algarotti, 'Lettera a Bernardo Fontenelle', 24 January 1736, in *Opere del conte Algarotti edizione novissima* (Venice, Carlo Palese, 1792), vol. ix, p. 17.
2 Melchiorre Cesarotti, 'Saggio sulla filosofia del gusto all'Arcadia di Roma', in *Opere scelte*, ed. G. Ortolani (Florence, Le Monnier, 1945), vol. i, p. 212.
3 Pietro Verri, 'Articoli tratti dal "Caffè"', in *Opere varie*, ed. N. Valeri, vol. i (Florence, Le Monnier, 1947), p. 35.
4 Ibid., p. 48.
5 Ibid., p. 70.
6 Ibid., p. 71.
7 Ibid., p. 9.
8 Ibid., pp. 50-1.
9 *Carteggio di Pietro e di Alessandro Verri dal 1766 al 1797*, vol. iv (Milan, Cogliati, 1919), p. 270.
10 Lorenzo Magalotti, 'Al Signore Francesco Redi', in *La donna immaginaria. Canzoniere del Conte Lorenzo Magalotti. Con altre di lui leggiadrissime composizioni inedite, raccolte e pubblicate da Gaetano Cambiagi* ... (Lucca, Stamperia di Gio. Riccomini, 1762), pp. 229-30.
11 Francesco Redi, *Lettere di Francesco Redi Patrizio aretino*, 2nd edn

(Florence, Gaetano Cambiagi, 1779), vol. i, p. 381. The letter was written in September 1689.
12 Quoted in Ferdinando Massai, *Lo 'Stravizzo' della Crusca del 12 settembre 1666 e l'origine del 'Bacco in Toscana' di Francesco Redi* (Rocca S. Casciano, Cappelli, 1916), p. 21.
13 Redi, *Lettere*, vol. i, p. 381.
14 Ibid., pp. 381–2. 'Apicius and Athene would upbraid me if I overlooked this other remark, even though it is not really to the purpose, that the brain of the dolphin is a very delicate victual, and that it is not in the slightest way surpassed by the brain of sucking-veal or any other kind prepared in even the best and most ingenious of kitchens; I would go so far as to say, from experience, that it is much better and more delicate and noble' ('Osservazioni intorno agli animali viventi che si trovano negli animali viventi', in *Opuscoli di storia naturale di Francesco Redi*, ed. C. Livi, Florence, Le Monnier, 1858, p. 429).
15 Redi, *Lettere*, vol. i, p. 382.
16 Ibid., pp. 382–3.

CHAPTER 6 THE STRANGE NEW ADOPTIONS OF LISTLESS GLUTTONY

1 Charles-Louis de Montesquieu, *Lettres persanes* (1765), p. 54.
2 Note written by eighteenth-century editor of *Lettere di Francesco Redi Patrizio aretino*, 2nd edn (Florence, Gaetano Cambiagi, 1779), vol. ii, p. 25.
3 Francesco Redi, letter to Diacinto Cestoni, 26 March 1680, in *Lettere*.
4 Francesco Redi, 'Esperienze intorno a diverse cose naturali e particolarmente a quelle che ci son portate dall'Indie', in *Opuscoli di storia naturale di Francesco Redi*, ed. C. Livi (Florence, Le Monnier, 1858), p. 287.
5 Ibid., p. 291.
6 This and the other extracts are taken from Lorenzo Magalotti, *Lettere familiari* [against atheism] (Venice, S. Coleti, 1732), pt i, p. 202.
7 Ibid.
8 Redi, 'Esperienze', p. 283.
9 Ibid.
10 Lorenzo Magalotti, 'Donde possa avvenire che nel giudizio degli odori così sovente si prenda abbaglio', addressed to Sig. Cavaliere

NOTES TO PAGES 57–62   169

Gio. Battista d'Ambra, in *Lettere sopra i buccheri con l'aggiunta di lettere contro l'ateismo, scientifiche e erudite e di relazioni varie*, ed. M. Praz (Florence, Le Monnier, 1945), p. 305.
11 Lorenzo Magalotti, 'Sopra il casciù', in *Lettere scientifiche ed erudite* (Venice, Domenico Occhi, 1740), p. 246.
12 Ibid., p. 244.
13 Ibid.
14 Ibid., p. 246.
15 Ibid., p. 247.
16 Magalotti, *Lettere familiari* [against atheism], pt i, p. 203.
17 [François de La Mothe le Vayer], *Cinq dialogues faits à l'imitation des Anciens. Par Oratio Tubero* (Liège, Gregoire Rousselin, 1673), p. 117. On the transition from Orasius to Oratius and the problem involved in dating the first edition, see René Pintard, 'Sur les débuts clandestins de La Mothe le Vayer: la publication des *Dialogues d'Orasius Tubero*', in *La Mothe le Vayer – Gassendi – Guy Patin. Etudes de bibliographie et critique suivies de textes inédites de Guy Patin* (Paris, Boivin et Cie. Editeurs, n.d.).
18 Part of an unpublished letter quoted by G. Tellini, 'Tre corrispondenti di Francesco Redi (lettere inedite di G. Montanari, F. D'Andrea, P. Boccone)', *Filologia e critica*, 1 (1976), p. 409, n. 10.
19 Gabriel-Honoré di Mirabeau, *Erotika Biblion. Édition revue et corrigée sur l'édition originale de 1783* . . . (Amsterdam, Aug. Brancart, 1890), p. 28.
20 Redi, 'Esperienze', p. 279.
21 Ibid., p. 280.
22 Francesco Redi, *Sei odi inedite di Francesco Redi* (Bologna, Romagnoli, 1864), p. 15.
23 [La Mothe le Vayer], *Cinq dialogues*, p. 123.
24 Ibid.
25 See Giuseppe Brofferio, *Cenno medico sull'uso della vipera e sopra un suo straordinario effetto* (Turin, Tipografia Chirio e Mina, 1822).
26 Giambattista Morgagni, *Consulti medici*, ed. E. Benassi (Bologna, Cappelli, 1935), p. 38.
27 Francesco Redi, *Consulti medici* (Turin, Boringhieri, 1958), p. 41.
28 Ibid., p. 57.
29 Francesco Redi, 'Osservazioni intorno alle vipere', in *Opuscoli di storia naturale*, pp. 40–1.
30 Ibid., p. 41.

31 Ibid.
32 Ibid.

CHAPTER 7 EPHEMERAL DÉCOR

1 Paolo Palliolo Fanese, *Le feste pel conferimento del patriziato romano a Giuliano e Lorenzo de' Medici*, ed. O. Guerrini (Bologna, Romagnoli, 1885), quoted in G. Mazzoni, 'Un convito solenne', in *In biblioteca, Appunti* (Bologna, Zanichelli, 1886), p. 271.
2 Ibid., p. 272.
3 Ibid., p. 275.
4 Lines by Giovanni Gerolamo Pazzi, quoted in L. Valmaggi, *I cicisbei, Contributo alla storia del costume italiano nel sec. XVIII*, ed. L. Piccioni (Turin, Chiantore, 1927), p. 171.
5 *Carteggio di Pietro e di Alessandro Verri dal 1766 al 1797*, vol. ii (Milan, Cogliati, 1910), p. 322.
6 Ibid.
7 Ibid.
8 Cesare Beccaria, 'Frammento sugli odori', in *Il Caffè*, ed. S. Romagnoli (Milan, Feltrinelli, 1960), p. 37.
9 Ibid., pp. 33–4.
10 Ibid.
11 Francesco Redi, *Lettere di Francesco Redi Patrizio aretino*, 2nd edn (Florence, Gaetano Cambiagi, 1779), vol. ii, p. 393.
12 Francesco Leonardi, *Apicio moderno ossia l'arte del credenziere* (Rome, Stamperia del Giunchi, Carlo Mordacchini, 1807), vol. ii, p. 83.
13 Ibid., vol. i, p. 3.
14 Ibid.
15 Ibid., pp. 4–5.
16 Ibid., p. 3.
17 Ibid., pp. 3–4.
18 Ibid., pp. 23, 25–6.
19 Ibid., p. 150.

CHAPTER 8 A BLISSFUL AND DRINKABLE ETERNITY

1 Lorenzo Magalotti, 'Per un sogno avuto di tornare di Fiandra in Italia per le poste nel Sollione', in *La donna immaginaria. Canzoniere del*

Conte Lorenzo Magalotti. Con altre di lui leggiadrissime composizioni inedite, raccolte e pubblicate da Gaetano Cambiagi . . . (Lucca, Stamperia di Gio. Riccomini, 1762), p. 228.
2 Lorenzo Magalotti, 'La sorbettiera', in Canzonette anacreontiche di Lindoro Elateo Pastore Arcade (Florence, Tartini and Franchi, 1723), p. 35.
3 Lorenzo Magalotti, 'Trionfo dei buccheri', in Lettere odorose di Lorenzo Magalotti (1693–1705), ed. E. Falqui (Milan, Bompiani, 1943), p. 305.
4 Ibid., p. 306.
5 Magalotti, 'La sorbettiera', pp. 34, 35.
6 Lorenzo Magalotti, 'Regalo d'un finimento di bucchero nero', in Lettere odorose, p. 321.
7 Lorenzo Magalotti, Lettere sopra i buccheri con l'aggiunta di lettere contro l'ateismo, scientifiche e erudite e di relazioni varie, ed. M. Praz (Florence, Le Monnier, 1945), p. 108.
8 Magalotti, 'Regalo', pp. 321–2.
9 Ibid., p. 322.
10 Lorenzo Magalotti, 'Buccheri neri', in Lettere odorose, p. 314.
11 Magalotti, Lettere sopra i buccheri, p. 95.
12 Lorenzo Magalotti, 'Il fiore d'arancio. Ditirambo intitolato La Madreselva', in Lettere odorose, p. 327.
13 Ibid., p. 326.
14 E. Falqui (ed.), In giro per le Corti d'Europa, Antologia della prosa diplomatica del Seicento italiano (Rome, Colombo, 1949), p. 489.
15 Ibid., p. 488.
16 Lorenzo Magalotti, 'Sopra il mogarino stradoppio detto del cuore, mandato secco a Londra', in Canzonette anacreontiche, p. 22.
17 Falqui, In giro per le Corti d'Europa, p. 489.
18 Ibid., p. 488.
19 Ibid.
20 Ibid., p. 491.
21 Ibid., p. 490.
22 Ibid., p. 493.
23 Ibid.
24 Ibid.
25 Ibid., pp. 494–5.
26 Ibid., p. 493.
27 Lorenzo Magalotti, 'La merenda', in Canzonette anacreontiche, pp. 62–3.

28 Lorenzo Magalotti, *Lettere del Conte Lorenzo Magalotti Gentiluomo fiorentino* (Florence, Giuseppe Manni, 1736), p. 43.
29 Magalotti, *Lettere sopra i buccheri*, p. 342.
30 Ibid.
31 Ibid., p. 343.
32 Lorenzo Magalotti, 'Frittata', in *Canzonette anacreontiche*, p. 69.
33 Magalotti, 'La merenda', p. 61.
34 Ibid., pp. 61–2.
35 Lorenzo Magalotti, *Lettere familiari* [against atheism] (Venice, S. Coleti, 1732), pt i, p. 317.
36 Ibid.
37 Ibid.
38 Ibid., p. 316.
39 Ibid.
40 Ibid., p. 300.
41 Ibid., p. 301.
42 Ibid.
43 Carlo Roberto Dati, 'Il cedrarancio. Selva', in *Prose*, ed. E. Allodoli (Carabba, Lanciano, 1913), p. 102.
44 Magalotti, *Lettere familiari* [against atheism], pt i, pp. 299–300.
45 Carlo Roberto Dati, 'Il cedrarancio. Veglia', in *Prose*, p. 81.
46 Dati, 'Il cedrarancio. Selva', p. 102.
47 Dati, 'Il cedrarancio. Veglia', p. 81.
48 Magalotti, *Lettere familiari* [against atheism], pt i, p. 301.
49 Magalotti, *Lettere del Conte*, p. 117.

CHAPTER 9 THE BOTANY OF THE PALATE

1 Pietro Verri, 'Articoli tratti dal "Caffè"', in *Opere varie*, ed. N. Valeri, vol. i (Florence, Le Monnier, 1947), p. 48.
2 Ibid.
3 Lorenzo Magalotti, *Lettere del Conte Lorenzo Magalotti Gentiluomo fiorentino* (Florence, Giuseppe Manni, 1736), pp. 136–7. This is also found in Lorenzo Magalotti, *Scritti di corte e di mondo*, ed. E. Falqui (Rome, Colombo, 1945), pp. 346–7. On 'Bu tea' see also Francesco Leonardi, *Apicio moderno ossia l'arte del credenziere* (Rome, Stamperia del Giunchi, Carlo Mordacchini, 1807), vol. ii, pp. 333–4.
4 Lorenzo Magalotti, *Lettere familiari* [against atheism] (Venice, S. Coleti, 1732), pt i, p. 202.

NOTES TO PAGES 85–91

5 Magalotti, *Lettere del Conte*, pp. 135–6; see also *Scritti di corte e di mondo*, p. 346.
6 Verri, 'Articoli tratti dal "Caffè"', p. 49.
7 Ibid., p. 48.
8 Ibid.
9 Leonardi, *Apicio moderno*, vol. i, p. 95.
10 Giuseppe Baretti, *Lettere familiari a' suoi fratelli* (Milan, Silvestri, 1836), p. 216.
11 Leonardi, *Apicio moderno*, vol. i, p. 260.
12 Ibid.
13 Jacques Delille, *Les jardins, ou l'art d'embellir les paysages. Poème, par M. l'abbé De Lille* (Paris, Valade, 1782), p. 93.
14 Francesco Algarotti, 'Lettere varie', in *Opere del conte Algarotti edizione novissima* (Venice, Carlo Palese, 1792), vol. ix, pp. 186–7.
15 Ibid., pp. 185–6.
16 Ibid., p. 187.
17 Saverio Bettinelli, 'Lettere a Lesbia Cidonia sopra gli epigrammi', in *Opere edite e inedite in prosa ed in versi dell'abate Saverio Bettinelli*, 2nd edn (Venice, Adolfo Cesare, 1799), vol. xxi, p. 39.
18 Leonardi, *Apicio moderno*, vol. i, p. 261.
19 Ibid., pp. 261–2.
20 *Carteggio di Pietro e di Alessandro Verri dal 1766 al 1797*, vol. iii (Milan, Cogliati, 1911), p. 19.
21 Francesco Algarotti, 'Pensieri diversi', in *Opere*, vol. vii, p. 235.
22 *Carteggio di Pietro e di Alessandro Verri*, vol. iii, p. 309.
23 Giuseppe Parini, 'Il Mattino', lines 80–4.
24 Algarotti, 'Lettere varie', pp. 164–5.
25 Girolamo Baruffaldi, 'Bacco in Giovecca', in *Baccanali*, 2nd edn (Bologna, Lelio dalla Volpe, 1758), vol. i, p. 11.
26 Giovambatista Roberti, 'Lettera ad un vecchio e ricco Signore feudatario sopra il lusso del secolo XVIII', in *Scelta di lettere erudite del padre Giovambatista Roberti* (Venice, Tipografia di Alvisopoli, 1825), p. 131.
27 Giovambatista Roberti, 'Lettera al Consigliere Gian-Lodovico Bianconi intorno alle sue opere sopra Celso', in *Scelta di lettere erudite*, pp. 164–6.
28 Ibid., p. 164.
29 Niccolò Carteromaco [Forteguerri], *Ricciardetto* (Lucca, 1766), vol. ii, p. 383 (canto xxx, 82–3).
30 Leonardi, *Apicio moderno*, vol. i, p. 249.

31 Filippo Re, *Nuovi elementi di agricoltura* (Milan, G. Silvestri, 1815), vol. iii, p. 176. On pears in the economy of Renaissance food, see Costanzo Felici, *Dell'insalata e piante che in qualunque modo vengono per cibo dell'homo*, letter-cum-treatise written for Ulisse Aldrovandi in 1568 and printed for the first time by G. Arbizzoni, Urbino, Quattro Venti, 1986. In particular, see pp. 91–3.
32 Vincenzo Tanara, *L'economia del cittadino in villa* (Venice, G. B. Tramontin, 1687), p. 344.
33 Leonardi, *Apicio moderno*, vol. i, p. 244.
34 *Il giardiniero francese, overo trattato del tagliare gl'alberi da frutto con la maniera di ben allevarli, trasportato dal francese di Monsù René Dahavron giardiniere del Serenissimo Duca di Bransuvich: aggiunto un compendio delle regole, e massime più necessarie per l'esercitio di quest'arte. Cavate da Monsù della Quintinyé Sopraintendente generale de' giardini di Sua Maestà Christianissima. Come pure accresciuto in questa seconda edizione della Instruzione per la coltura de' fiori dello stesso Monsù della Quintinié* (Venice, Girolamo Albrizzi, 1704), pp. 50–5.
35 See *Agrumi, frutta e uve nella Firenze di Bartolomeo Bimbi pittore mediceo* (Florence, Consiglio Nazionale delle Ricerche, 1982), pp. 104–22. The investigation was promoted by E. Baldini and F. Scaramuzzi.
36 Ibid., p. 115.
37 Saverio Bettinelli, 'Risorgimento d'Italia negli studi, nelle arti e nei costumi dopo il Mille' (1755), in *Opere edite e inedite*, vol. x, p. 264.
38 Ibid.
39 Ibid., pp. 264–6.
40 Ibid., p. 261.
41 Ibid.
42 Ibid., p. 258.
43 Ibid., p. 259.
44 Ibid., p. 258.
45 Giuseppe Colpani, 'Il gusto', in *Poemetti italiani* (Turin, Società Letteraria di Torino, Michel Angelo Morano, 1797), vol. ii, p. 104.
46 Ibid.
47 Ibid., p. 116.
48 Ibid., p. 104.
49 Ibid., p. 106.
50 Ibid., p. 104.
51 Ibid., pp. 104–5.
52 Pietro Verri, 'Discorso sull'indole del piacere e del dolore', in *Del piacere e del dolore ed altri scritti di filosofia ed economia*, ed. R. De Felice

(Milan, Feltrinelli, 1964), p. 44.
53 Ibid.
54 Ibid., p. 45.

CHAPTER 10 PERFIDIOUS ART

1 Giovambatista Roberti, 'Annotazioni sopra la Umanità del secolo decimottavo', in *Raccolta di varie operette dell'Abate Conte Giovambatista Roberti* (Bologna, Lelio dalla Volpe, 1785), vol. v, p. liii.
2 Ibid., pp. xliv−xlvi.
3 Ibid., pp. xv−xvi.
4 Giovambatista Roberti, 'Lettera ad un vecchio e ricco Signore feudatario sopra il lusso del secolo XVIII', in *Scelta di lettere erudite del padre Giovambatista Roberti* (Venice, Tipografia di Alvisopoli, 1825), pp. 123−4.
5 Joseph de Maistre, *Les soirées de Saint-Pétersbourg ou entretiens sur le gouvernement temporel de la Providence* (Brussels, Meline, Cans et Cie., 1837), p. 62.
6 Roberti, 'Annotazioni sopra la Umanità', pp. cxvii−cxviii.
7 Roberti, 'Lettera ad un vecchio e ricco Signore feudatario', p. 136 and *passim*.
8 Francesco Algarotti, 'Epistole in versi', in *Opere del conte Algarotti edizione novissima* (Venice, Carlo Palese, 1792), vol. i, p. 50: 'A Lesbia'.
9 Roberti, 'Lettera ad un vecchio e ricco Signore feudatario', p. 142.
10 Ibid., pp. 142−3.
11 Ibid., pp. 127−8.
12 Ibid., p. 127.
13 Lorenzo Magalotti, 'Relazione d'Inghilterra dell'anno 1668', in *Relazioni di viaggio in inghilterra Francia e Svezia*, ed. W. Moretti (Bari, Laterza, 1968), pp. 56−7.
14 Giovambatista Roberti, 'Lettera sopra i fiori', in *Raccolta di operette dell'Abate Conte*, vol. iv, pp. vi−vii.
15 Pietro Chiari, 'De' cibi appruovati, e disappruovati dall'uso', in *Lettere scelte di varie materie piacevoli, critiche, ed erudite scritte ad una dama di qualità* (Venice, Angelo Pasinelli, 1751), vol. ii, p. 209.
16 Ibid., pp. 209−12.
17 Ibid., pp. 212−13.
18 Roberti, 'Lettera ad un vecchio e ricco Signore feudatario', p. 125.

19 Ibid.
20 Roberti, 'Lettera sopra i fiori', p. iv.
21 Ibid.
22 Ibid., p. viii.
23 Giovambatista Roberti, 'Lettera di un bambino di sedici mesi colle annotazioni di un filosofo', in *Raccolta di varie operette del padre Giovambatista Roberti della Compagnia di Gesù* (Bologna, Lelio dalla Volpe, 1767), vol. ii, p. lxxiii.

CHAPTER 11 INDIAN BROTH

1 Francesco Redi, 'Annotazioni di Francesco Redi al Ditirambo', in *Opere di Francesco Redi* (Milan, Società tipografica de' classici italiani, 1809), vol. i, p. 74.
2 Francesco Redi, *Lettere di Francesco Redi Patrizio aretino*, 2nd edn (Florence, Gaetano Cambiagi, 1779), vol. ii, p. 32.
3 Ibid.
4 Francesco Redi, *Scelta di lettere familiari di Francesco Redi* (Venice, Girolamo Tasso, 1846), p. 186.
5 Ibid., p. 189.
6 Ibid., p. 187.
7 Redi, 'Annotazioni al Ditirambo', pp. 78–9.
8 Giuseppe Girolamo Semenzi, *Il Mondo Creato diviso nelle sette giornate. Poesie mistiche del P. D. Giuseppe Girolamo Semenzi Chierico Regolare Somasco Professore di Sacra Teologia nella Regia Università di Pavia* (Milan, Carlo Antonio Malatesta, 1686), p. 196.
9 Ibid.
10 See Wolfgang Schivelbush, *Das Paradies, der Geschmack und die Vernunft. Il paradiso, il gusto e il buonsenso. Una storia dei generi voluttuari* (Bari and Rome, De Donato, 1988).
11 'There is no counting the money that Europeans nowadays spend on cocoa and on other chocolate drugs. Dr Crescenzio Vaselli, from Siena, as worthy of respect for his civility as for his erudition, cautiously drew attention to this fact in a letter that he wrote to me not long ago, saying that "if there were no other reason for pursuing and outlawing chocolate, it ought to be done on political grounds alone: after all, there is no lack of household and natural things able to excite our greed without suspicion of danger." (*Parere intorno all'uso della cioccolata scritto in una lettera dal Conte Dottor Gio. Battista Felici*

all'illustrissima Signora Lisabetta Girolami D'Ambra, Florence, Giuseppe Manni, 1728, p. 67).
12 Semenzi, *Il Mondo Creato*, p. 194. One of the earliest narrators of the 'medical history of coffee' was Count Luigi Ferdinando Marsili who, on being taken prisoner by Turks, was obliged, as a slave, 'for many days in a smoke-filled tent to exercise the art of cooking coffee'. See his *Bevanda asiatica* (Vienna, Gio. Van Ghelen, 1685), recently republished (Bologna, 1986) in a critical edition, with a learned commentary by Clemente Mazzotta. Marsili believed that coffee, among its other powers, possessed that of 'making the mind clear' (Vienna edn, p. 46).
13 Marcello Malaspina, 'Bacco in America', in *Raccolta di varij poemetti lirici, drammatici e ditirambici degli Arcadi* (Rome, Antonio de' Rossi, 1722), vol. ix of *Rime*, pp. 381–2.
14 Adelasto Anascalio, 'Intorno la cioccolata', in *Saggio di lettere piacevoli, critiche, morali, scientifiche e instruttive in versi martelliani* (Venice, Marcellino Piotto, 1759), p. 97.
15 Pietro Metastasio, 'La cioccolata', in *Tutte le opere di Pietro Metastasio*, ed. B. Brunelli (Milan, Mondadori, 1965), vol. ii, p. 729.
16 John Philips, 'Il Sidro', trans. Count Lorenzo Magalotti, 2nd edn (Florence, Andrea Bonducci, 1752); 1st edn Florence, 1744.
17 Lorenzo Magalotti, 'Il Sidro', in *Canzonette anacreotiche di Lindoro Elateo Pastore Arcade* (Florence, Tartini and Franchi, 1723), p. 80.
18 Girolamo Baruffaldi, 'Le nozze saccheggiate', in *Baccanali*, 2nd edn (Bologna, Lelio dalla Volpe, 1758), vol. i, p. 36.
19 Giovanni Dallabona, *Dell'uso e dell'abuso del caffè. Dissertazione storico-fisico-medica del dottor G. D. Seconda edizione con aggiunte, massime intorno la cioccolata ed il rosoli*, 2nd edn (Verona, Pierantonio Berno, 1760), p. 81.
20 Francesco Arisi, *Il Cioccolato. Trattenimento ditirambico di Francesco Arisi, Eufemo Batio tra gli Arcadi* (Cremona, Stamperia di Pietro Ricchini, 1736), pp. 8–10.
21 Ibid., p. 6.
22 Ibid., pp. 6–7.
23 Francesco Redi, 'Esperienze intorno a diverse cose naturali e particolarmente a quelle che ci son portate dall'Indie', in *Opuscoli di storia naturale di Francesco Redi*, ed. C. Livi (Florence, Le Monnier, 1858), pp. 236–7.
24 Lorenzo Magalotti, *Lettere familiari* [against atheism] (Venice, S. Coleti, 1732), pt i, p. 126.

25 Ibid.
26 Ibid., p. 130.
27 Francesco Redi, letter to Diacinto Marmi, 25 February 1683, in *Scelta di lettere familiari*, p. 142. See Redi's *Consulti medici e opuscoli minori*, ed. C. Livi (Florence, Le Monnier, 1863), p. 205: 'Many patients and many doctors often fall into the mistaken opinion that the stomach is cold and the liver hot. The most ridiculous thing, it seems to me, is that they blame the coldness of the poor old stomach on the excessive heat of the insolent liver and that they advance arguments and reasons that would be shocking if heard from the lips of old wives, sitting on winter evenings telling tales to their grandchildren.'
28 Magalotti, *Lettere familiari* [against atheism], pt i, pp. 11–12.
29 Ibid., p. 130.
30 Francesco Redi, 'Bacco in Toscana', in *Opere*, vol. i, p. 10. *Translator's note*: I have used the lively contemporary translation by Leigh Hunt: *Bacchus in Tuscany. A Dithyrambic Poem, from the Italian of Francesco Redi with notes original and select* (London, 1785). The last four lines of the passage would read more accurately, but also more prosaically: 'Bring me heaps from the Shady Valley / Snow aplenty / Bring it from every hilltop hovel / A great abundance of snow . . .'
31 Redi, 'Annotazioni al Ditirambo', pp. 120–1.
32 Baruffaldi, 'Le nozze saccheggiate', p. 40.

CHAPTER 12 MAD AND STARTLING NAMES

1 Lorenzo Bellini, *La bucchereide* (Bologna, Masi, 1823), pt i, proem ii, p. 154, octave 98, line 3.
2 Francesco Redi, 'Bacco in Toscana', in *Opere di Francesco Redi* (Milan, Società tipografica de' classici italiani, 1809), vol. i, pp. 18–19; Eng. trans. by Leigh Hunt as *Bacchus in Tuscany. A Dithyrambic Poem, from the Italian of Francesco Redi with notes original and select* (London, 1785), p. 33.
3 Bellini, *La bucchereide*, pt i, proem ii, pp. 154–5, octaves 99–101.
4 Giovambatista Roberti, 'Lettera di un bambino di sedici mesi colle annotazioni di un filosofo', in *Raccolta di varie operette del padre Giovambatista Roberti della Compagnia di Gesù* (Bologna, Lelio dalla Volpe, 1767), vol. ii, p. lxxiii.
5 See Krzysztof Pomian, *Collectionneurs, amateurs et curieux. Paris, Venise: XVIe–XVIIIe siècle* (Paris, Gallimard, 1987); Eng. trans. *Collectors and*

Curiosities (Cambridge, Polity Press, 1990).
6 Bellini, *La bucchereide*, pt ii, proem ii, pp. 18–19, octaves 39–40.
7 Ibid., pt i, proem ii, p. 155, octave 103.
8 Ibid., pt ii, proem ii, p. 25, octave 65.
9 Ibid., octave 66.
10 Ibid., pt i, proem i, pp. 97–8.
11 Lorenzo Magalotti, *Lettere sopra i buccheri con l'aggiunta di lettere contro l'ateismo, scientifiche e erudite e di relazioni varie*, ed. M. Praz (Florence, Le Monnier, 1945), p. 306.
12 Bellini, *La bucchereide*, 'Cicalata del dottor Lorenzo Bellini per servir di proemio alla Bucchereide, recitata nell'Accademia della Crusca per lo Stravizzo del dì 13 settembre dell' anno 1699', pp. 68–9.
13 Francesco Redi, *Scelta di lettere familiari di Francesco Redi* (Venice, Girolamo Tasso, 1846), p. 145.
14 Giuseppe Averani, 'Delle lodi del conte Magalotti nell'Accademia della Crusca detto il Sollevato. Orazione funerale di Giuseppe Averani detta nell'Accademia della Crusca il dì 18 agosto 1712', in *Lezioni toscane di varia letteratura*, 2nd edn (Florence, Gaetano Albrizzini, 1766), pp. 253, 255.
15 Magalotti, *Lettere sopra i buccheri*, pp. 310–11.

CHAPTER 13 QUINTESSENCES OF JUICES

1 Giovambatista Roberti, 'La moda', in *Raccolta di varie operette del padre Giovambatista Roberti della Compagnia di Gesù* (Bologna, Lelio dalla Volpe, 1767), vol. i, p. xxi, octave ix.
2 Ibid.
3 Ibid., p. xxx, octave xxvii.
4 Francesco Algarotti, 'Epistole in versi', in *Opere del conte Algarotti edizione novissima* (Venice, Carlo Palese, 1792), vol. i, p. 9: 'Alla Maestà di Augusto III. Re di Polonia, Elettor di Sassonia'.
5 Roberti, 'La moda', p. xxii, octave x.
6 Algarotti, 'Epistole in versi', p. 11: 'A Pietro Grimani. Doge di Venezia'.
7 Roberti, 'La moda', p. xxii, octave x.
8 Giovambatista Roberti, 'Lettera ad un vecchio e ricco Signore feudatario sopra il lusso del secolo XVIII', in *Scelta di lettere erudite del padre Giovambatista Roberti* (Venice, Tipografia di Alvisopoli, 1825), p. 129.

9 Ibid., p. 126.
10 Ibid.
11 Ibid.
12 Ibid., p. 129.
13 Ibid., p. 130.
14 Ibid., pp. 126–7.
15 Ibid., p. 129.
16 Ibid.
17 Ibid.
18 Ibid.
19 Ibid.
20 Ibid.
21 *Carteggio di Pietro e di Alessandro Verri dal 1766 al 1797*, vol. iii (Milan, Cogliati, 1911), p. 308.
22 Ibid., p. 309.
23 Giuseppe Averani, *Lezioni toscane di varia letteratura*, 2nd edn (Florence, Gaetano Albrizzini, 1766), vol. iii, p. 73.
24 *Carteggio di Pietro e di Alessandro Verri*, vol. vi (1928), p. 25.
25 Johann Joachim Winckelmann, *Lettere italiane*, ed. G. Zampa (Milan, Feltrinelli, 1961), p. 93.
26 *Carteggio di Pietro e di Alessandro Verri*, vol. vii (1931), p. 260.
27 Ibid., vol. ii (1910), p. 191.
28 Roberti, 'Lettera ad un vecchio e ricco Signore feudatario', pp. 111–12.
29 *Carteggio di Pietro e di Alessandro Verri*, vol. vii, p. 66.
30 Ibid., p. 198.
31 Ibid., vol. vi, p. 183.

CHAPTER 14 THE LAVISH TABLE

1 Jean-Baptiste Labat, *La comédie ecclésiastique. Voyage en Espagne et en Italie* (Paris, Grasset, 1927), p. 133.
2 Giovambatista Roberti, 'Lettera al Nobil Signore Jacopo Vittorelli', in *Raccolta di varie operette dell'Abate Conte Giovambatista Roberti* (Bologna, Lelio dalla Volpe, 1785), vol. iv, p. xxxiv.
3 Ibid., pp. xxxii–xxxiii.
4 Francesco Leonardi, *Gianina ossia La Cuciniera delle Alpi* (Rome, 1817), vol. i, p. 96.
5 Ibid.

6 A. Bassani and G. Roversi, *Eminenza, il pranzo è servito. Le ricette di Alberto Alvisi cuoco del card. Chiaramonti vescovo di Imola (1785–1800)*, preface by P. Camporesi (Bologna, Aniballi, 1984), p. 175.
7 *Carteggio di Pietro e di Alessandro Verri dal 1766 al 1797*, vol. v (Milan, Cogliati, 1926), p. 65.
8 Ibid., pp. 100–1.
9 Pier Jacopo Martello, 'Lo starnuto di Ercole', in *Seguito del teatro italiano di Pier Jacopo Martello*, final pt (Bologna, Lelio dalla Volpe, 1723), p. 247.
10 Pier Jacopo Martello, 'Il vero parigino italiano', *Seguito del teatro italiano*, final pt, p. 318.
11 'Lettera del cav. Benvenuto Robbio Conte di S. Rafaele al padre Giovambatista Roberti', in *Scelta di lettere erudite del padre Giovambatista Roberti* (Venice, Tipografia di Alvisopoli, 1825), p. 204.
12 Giovambatista Roberti, 'Lettera sulla semplicità elegante', in *Scelta di lettere erudite*, p. 100.
13 Giovambatista Roberti, 'Risposta del padre Giovambatista Roberti al Conte di S. Rafaele', in *Scelta di lettere erudite*, pp. 222–4.
14 Ibid., p. 220.
15 Ibid., pp. 220–1.
16 Clemente Bondi, 'Il cioccolato', in *Poemetti e rime varie* (Venice, Gaspare Storti, 1778), p. 122.
17 Gioan-Ignazio Molina, 'Sul cacao', in *Memorie di storia naturale lette in Bologna nelle adunanze dell'Istituto* (Bologna, Tipografia Marsigli, 1821), pt ii, pp. 197–9.
18 Ibid., p. 211.
19 Roberti, 'Risposta al Conte di S. Rafaele', p. 219.
20 Giovambatista Roberti, 'Lettera ad un vecchio e ricco Signore feudatario sopra il lusso del secolo XVIII', in *Scelta di lettere erudite*, pp. 123–4.
21 Clemente Bondi, 'L'asinata', in *Poemetti e rime varie*, canto ii, octave ii, p. 63.
22 Ibid., octave xx, p. 68.
23 Francesco Algarotti, letter to Abbot Bettinelli, 1753, in *Opere del conte Algarotti edizione novissima* (Venice, Carlo Palese, 1792), vol. xiv, p. 88.
24 Niccolò Carteromaco [Forteguerri], *Ricciardetto* (Lucca, 1766), vol. ii, p. 208.
25 Ibid.
26 *Le Président de Brosses en Italie. Lettres familières écrites d'Italie en 1739 et*

1740 par Charles de Brosses, 2nd edn (Paris, Didier, 1858), vol. ii, pp. 168–9.
27 Ibid., p. 169.
28 Ibid., vol. ii, p. 22.
29 Ibid.
30 Ibid., p. 14.
31 Ibid., pp. 14–15.
32 Ibid., pp. 84–5.
33 Ibid., p. 86.
34 Ibid., p. 228.
35 *Carteggio di Pietro e di Alessandro Verri*, vol. vi (1928), p. 1.
36 *Le Président de Brosses en Italie*, vol. ii, p. 439.
37 Ibid., p. 20.
38 Ibid., p. 21.
39 Ibid., pp. 20–1.
40 Ibid., p. 21.
41 Ibid., p. 22.
42 Francesco Redi, *Consulti medici e opuscoli minori*, ed. C. Livi (Florence, Le Monnier, 1863). The other quotations from Redi are taken from *Consulti*, pp. 196, 186, 182. The two lines of verse are from the dithyramb 'Arianna inferma'.
43 *Le Président de Brosses en Italie*, vol. ii, p. 22.
44 Martello, 'Il vero parigino italiano', p. 298.
45 Ibid., pp. 312–13.
46 Ibid., p. 313.
47 Ibid., pp. 314–15.
48 Ibid., p. 315. We maintain the reading 'they would be lost' in preference to 'they would despair' suggested by Hannibal S. Noce in the edition of 'Il vero parigino italiano' published in *Scritti critici e satirici* by P. J. Martello (Bari, Laterza, 1963), p. 339.
49 Giovanni Lodovico Bianconi, 'Lettere sopra alcune particolarità della Baviera ed altri paesi della Germania', in *Letterati memorialisti e viaggiatori del Settecento*, ed. E. Bonora (Milan and Naples, Ricciardi, 1951), p. 924.
50 Jacques Delille, *Les jardins, ou l'art d'embellir les paysages. Poème, par M. L'abbé De Lille* (Paris, Valade, 1782), p. 94.
51 Ibid.
52 Ibid., p. 92.
53 Ibid., p. 93.
54 Ibid.

55 Roberti, 'Risposta al Conte di S. Rafaele', p. 219.
56 Martello, 'Il vero parigino italiano', p. 318.
57 Pier Jacopo Martello, 'Lettera a Ubertino Lando, patrizio piacentino', preface to 'Lo starnuto di Ercole', p. 245.
58 Ibid., p. 247.
59 Martello, 'Il vero parigino italiano', p. 325.
60 Roberti, 'Risposta al Conte di S. Rafaele', p. 217.
61 'Lettera del cav. Benvenuto Robbio Conte al padre Giovambatista Roberti', p. 20.
62 Ibid., p. 209.
63 Francesco Leonardi, *Apicio moderno ossia l'arte del credenziere* (Rome, Stamperia del Giunchi, Carlo Mordacchini, 1807), vol. i, p. 186.
64 Giovambatista Roberti, 'Le fragole', in *Raccolta di varie operette del padre Giovambatista Roberti della Compagnia di Gesù* (Bologna, Lelio dalla Volpe, 1767), vol. i, canto ii, octaves xxii–xxv, pp. 54–5.
65 Leonardi, *Apicio moderno*, vol. ii, p. 137.
66 Ibid., pp. 130–1, 131–2.

INDEX

abstinence 98
   from meat 7–8
Acosta, Giuseppe 143
Acquaviva, Cardinal of Aragona 148
'adornments of life' 23
Alfieri, Vittorio 25
Algarotti, Count Francesco 7, 37, 145
   on the Chinese 87
   on the French 2–3
   on pineapples 86
   on Voltaire 8
   on wine 88, 90
Alvisi, Alberto 140
amber 43, 64, 102, 103
animals
   fed on viper meat 60–1
   improving by cross-breeding 93
   introduction of new species 79–80
Anne, Queen of England 76–7
anorexia 105
apothecaries 150

appetite, lack of 100, 101-2, 104–5
Appiani, Father Paolo Antonio 110
apples, scent of 65
apricots 82, 93
archaeology 134
architecture
   airy sugar-built feats of 68–9, 159
   of the Enlightenment 4, 36
   French 152–3, 154–5
   Italian 149, 151–2, 154
Arisi, Francesco 117
Aristotelian philosophy, decline of 46–7
Artusi, Pellegrino 49
asparagus 83
Augustus, Emperor 33
Averani, Giuseppe 133

banquets 10, 28
Baretti, Giuseppe 85, 155
Barholin, Thomas 119
baroque age
   cookery 99–100

INDEX

enemas and purges   117–18
   meals   130–1
   and viper meat   61–2
   women   102
Baruffaldi, Girolamo   88
Bassano, Count and Abbot of   89
Beccaria, Cesare   66–7
beggars   97
Bellini, Lorenzo   122, 126–7
Benedict XIV, Pope   97, 148–9
Benzoni, Girolamo   143
Bergerac, Cyrano de   110
Berni, Francesco   110
Bettinelli, Abbot Saverio   9, 86, 96, 97, 145
   Diagloghi d'Amore   3-5
beverages *see* drinks
Bianconi, Giovanni Lodovico   89, 153–4
birds' nests   56
Bologna   141, 142, 156
   and middle-class cuisine   25–6
   poverty of peasants in   96–7
Bonaventuri, Tommaso   19
Bondi, Clemente   142, 144–5
Borromée, Monsignor Vitaliano, Vice-Legate of Bologna   139
brains
   dolphins'   51
   fallow-deer   50–2
Braudel, F.   13, 49
Brosses, Charles de   146–9, 151
Bu tea   84
buffets   65, 69–70, 136–7, 159–60
bulimia   105

cabbage, banning of   37, 48, 65

Candiero, recipe in verse for   42
cantimplora   121
Capacelli, Marquis Francesco Albergati   2, 21
Caraffa, Cardinal   2
Carême, Antoinin   28, 29–30
Casanova, Giacomo   134, 135
Castiglione, Monsignor Sabba   13
Catherine of Braganza, Queen   102, 103
Catherine II, Tsarina of Russia (the Great)   9, 10
Catholic circles/religious orders on the changes in eighteenth-century society   14–16
   and chocolate   111–13
cedrarancio (lemon/orange cross)   81
'century of gold'   93
'century of iron'   93
Cestoni, Diancinto   54, 109
chacuterie   155–6
champagne   140
Chardin, Jean   87
Charles II, King of England   90, 102
cheese
   banning of   37, 48, 65
   smell of   65, 66
cherries, Morello   119
'Chiapa pepper' (*Pimienta de Chapas*)   54–5
Chiaramonti, Barnabas   140
Chiari, Abbot Pietro   103–5
chicory   93
Chigi, Prince   136–7
China   53, 87
Chinese fennel   55

INDEX

Chinese porcelain 82, 112
chocolate 43, 55, 73–4, 83,
    108–14, 130, 140–4
  baroque 108
  cocoa 55, 112, 115–17, 121
  Enlightenment 108
  immersed in a sea of 157
  jasmine-flavoured 45, 108,
    109–11
  sorbet 72
  in Spain 45
  and sugar 157, 158
cider 114–15
citrus essences 84–5
cleanliness, improvements in
    personal 94, 96
Clement XII, Pope 148
  violet dinner given by 146–7
Clement XIII, Pope 133
clothes 4, 5, 24
  men's 4, 17, 36
clysters 45
cocoa 55, 112, 115-17, 121
  Soconosco 142
coffee 47, 48, 83, 86, 112, 114,
    117, 121, 130
cold drinks 117, 118, 121
colours of food 6–7
compotes 67, 87
Condillac, Abbot Etienne Bonnot
    de 99, 134
confectionary 65, 68, 102, 103
content (recipe from England)
    42–3
'convulsive aura' 65
cookery books 27–8, 33–4
cooks, compared with potters
    104
Corsini, Cardinal 145
crockery 68

Cussy, Marquis de 29

Dahayron (Dahuron), René 92
D'Ambra, Giovanni Battista
    122–5
Dati, Carlo Roberto 81
deer
  fallow-deer brains 50–2
  slaughtering of 50
Del Lago, Dr Iacopo 51
Delille, Jacques 155
desserts 159–60
Di San Rafaele, Count
    Benvenuto di 141, 156–7
Di Sangro, Raimondo 132–3
dining rooms 153
diseases 94
doctors 144, 150
dogs, new crossbreeds 80
dolphins' brains 51
drinking, separation from eating
    32
drinks 71, 100
  chilled and iced 68, 71, 121
  cocoa 112, 115–17, 121
  cold 117, 118, 121
  hot 100, 117, 121
  ice combined with wine
    120–1
  soft 83
  'visual swigs' 119–20
Dubos, Abbot, Canon of
    Beauvais 99

eating
  alone 31–2
  with lack of appetite 100,
    101–2, 104–5
  obsessive eating habits 62
  separation from drinking 32

INDEX 187

effeminacy 14, 16–17, 27
enemas 117, 118
England 44, 90
Epicureanism 23
Epicurus 39, 40
Ercolani, Filippo 153

fallow-deer brains 50–2
fans 19–20
fasting 98, 146
   culinary deceptions during periods of 59
   see also abstinence
fever attacks 119–20
fickleness 23
figs 80, 86, 119, 120, 148
fish, meats disguised as 59
flowers 75–7, 92
   jasmine 76–7, 82, 155
   paintings of 81, 82
   roses 75–6
Fontenelle, Bernard Le Bovier de 99
food
   changes in the Enlightenment era 4–8, 47–53, 99–100, 138–9
   discrimination against foods considered vulgar 65
   over-elaborate cooking and refinement of 103–5
   to appeal to the eye 6–7, 106
foreign influences in Italy 97–8
France
   architecture 152–3, 154–5
   compared with Italy 148–55
   exports of finery 20
   fashions in flowers 76
   French customs and fashions in Tuscany 67

French influence on Italian cuisine 1–3, 27–31, 32–4
Italian dishes tasted by Frenchmen 144
Magalotti in 44–5
and new plants from Holland 92–3
and pears 92
'service à la français' 67–8
Frederick II, King of Prussia (the Great) 2, 8, 86, 87, 131
French Revolution 99
Frugoni, Carlo Innocenzo 2, 106, 132
Frugoni, Francesco Fulvio 58
fruit 83, 93, 148
   cedrarancio 81
   grapes 83, 148
   melons 83, 86, 148
   out of season 104
   paintings of 81, 82, 91
   pears 91–2, 93
   pineapples 83, 85–7, 155
   strawberries 119
furniture 4, 36

Galiani, Abbot Ferdinando 7–8, 103
Galileo Galilei 51
game 5, 40, 80
Ganganelli, Pope 135–6
gardens 85, 95
   artificial 106–7, 159
   at Bellevue 154
garlic, banning of 37, 65
'geometry of the spirit' 7
ginseng 55
Giuseppe del Bosco, Prince 92
gluttony 80

Goa 76
grafting of plants 80–1
grapes 83, 148
Grossi, Pier Luigi 16, 22
Guiducci, Niccolò 92

hairdressers 34, 66
Hazard, Paul 1
Heliogabalus, Emperor 133
Henri II, King of France 33
herbs 83, 93, 150
Holland
  creation of new plants by
    92–3
  Eastern and Caribbean imports
    83–4
  exports of linen 20
honeysuckle 76
Honour, Hugh 114
Horace 39
horse-riding 9, 10
hot drinks 117, 121
hothouses 85, 86, 155
houses 94
Hungarian wine 88, 89
hunts 40, 50
husbands 12, 17
hypochondria 65, 94

ice, combined with wine 120–1
ice-cream 70, 72–3, 117
  see also sorbets
iced chocolate 72, 117
iced drinks 68, 71, 121
illnesses 94
imaginary meals 130
imaginary tastiness 57–8
imitations of dishes 133
India, delicacies from 74
Indian jasmine 76–7

indigestion 7–8
Isabella, Infanta of Spain 45

James I, King of England 118
jasmine 76–7, 82, 155
jasmine-flavoured chocolate 45,
  108, 109–11
jellies 85
jesters 64
Jesuits
  and chocolate 110–11, 113
  trading by 55

kitchen arrangements 152

La Mothe le Vayer, François 58,
  61
La Quintinyé, Monseigneur de
  92
La Toletta 18
Labat, Friar G. B. 138
Laguipierre, Maître 28
Lambertini, Cardinal 147
lamb's testicles 77
'lamp-women' 13
Lanzoni, Giuseppe 133
lapdogs 80
lazy living 24, 27
Leghorn 54
lemonade 71, 83
Leonardi, Francesco 60, 69–71
  on the buffet 159–60
  on pineapples 85, 86, 87
  on sauces 140
Leopardi, Giacomo, *Zibaldone*
  31–2
Leopold, Prince 81
Leopoldo, Pietro 76
lettuce 83, 93
libertinism 102

liqueurs 70–1, 84–5
listlessness 80
Litta, Alessandro, Bishop of Cremona 117
liver (human organ) 119
Louis XIV, King of France 29, 131
Louis XV, King of France 106
Louis XVI, King of France 40

Magalotti, Lorenzo 39, 41–5, 80
  'Al Signore Francesco Redi' 49–50
  on Bu tea 83–4
  on Cardinal Moncada's perfumed *Boveda* 41–2
  on Catherine of Braganza 102
  and the *cedrarancio* 81
  and 'Chiapa pepper' 54–5
  and chocolate 111
  on chocolate 73
  and cider 115
  on fans 19–20
  on foreign flowers and fruit 80–1
  and the Indian jasmine 76–7
  on liqueurs 84–5
  on the liver 119
  on new animal species 79–80
  on omelettes 77–9
  on oysters 40
  and paintings 81–2
  and smells 126, 127–8
  on sophisticated palates 56–7
  travels 44–5
  on 'visual swigs' 119–20
  and 'water of cachou' 57
  on wine 90–1

maidenhair ferns 76
Maintenon, Madame de 131
Maistre, Count Joseph de 98
Marie Antoinette, Queen of France 40, 76
Martello, Pier Iacopo 141, 151, 153, 156
Massailot 27, 37
meat
  abstinence from 7–8
  ban on 'heavy and vicious meats' 47, 49, 65
  banishment of black meats 39, 40
  decline in consumption of 49
  masquerading as fish 59
Medici, Cosimo I 81
Medici, Cosimo III 42, 44, 52, 67-8, 76, 77, 92, 102, 115
  and chocolate 108–9, 110
Medici, Queen Catherine de 33
medieval age, compared with the Enlightenment era 3–7
melons 83, 86, 148
Mengs, Anton Raphael 133, 134
Mengs, Margherita Guazzi de 134
'merenades' (afternoon treats) 77–9
Mexico 74
Micheli, Pietro Antonio 92
middle-class cuisine 25–6
modesty 22
Molina, Gion-Ignazio 144
Moncada, Cardinal Luigi Guglielmo 41–2, 45, 118
Montaigne, Michel Eyquem de 2–3

Montesquieu, Charles Louis de
  12, 32, 54, 87
  'Essai sur le goût' 13
  and *politesse* 31
Morellet, Abbot 8
Morello cherries 119
Morgagni, Giovan Battista 61
Morgan, Lady 29
mortadella 156
musk 64, 102, 103

night, lifting of taboo of the
  12–13
'noble banquets' (*stravizzi*) 126,
  132
noses 66, 110, 123, 124, 126,
  127
novelty, love of 22–3

obsessive eating habits 62
omelettes 77–9
onions, banning of 37, 65
orange-flowers
  fragrant omelette of 78–9
  scent of 65
orangeade 71, 83
Orléans, Marguerite Louise d'
  68, 77
Orléans, Philippe d', Regent of
  France 30
oysters, growing popularity of
  39–40

paintings
  Chinese 87
  of flowers 81, 82
  of fruit 81, 82, 91
  of natural subjects 81
palates, sophisticated 56–7
Panciatichi, Lorenzo 81

Parini, Giuseppe 1–2
  'La Notte' 12
Parma 17, 87
Passionei, Cardinal Domenico
  135, 147
pastries 65
pastry-cookery 29–30, 33–4
'patriarchal' dishes, of the old
  society 6, 36, 37
peaches 86, 93
peacock 49–50
pears 91–2, 93
peasants 96–7
Pelargonium triste (Indian
  pelargonium) 81
perfumes 66
Persia 87
Petrarch 3–5
Petronius 39
Philips, John, 'The Cider' 115
philosophy, decline of Aristotelian
  46–7
Piedmontese pastry-making
  33–4
Pierre, François, Sieur de La
  Varenne 27
Pietro Leopoldo I, Grand Duke
  of Tuscany 134
Pighetti, Count 156
Pimienta de Chapas ('Chiapa
  pepper') 54–5
pineapples 83, 85–7, 155
Pintard, René 61
plant grafts 80–1
Pliny 60
polenta 145
politesse 31
Polyphagus 58
Pompadour, Madame de 106,
  154

porcelain   82, 112, 129
pork   155
Portugal   76, 85
potato flowers   76
poverty, of peasants in Bologna
    96–7
Protestant ethic, and coffee   112
purges   117–18, 119
pusu   55

quality of life, improvement in
    94
quinine   55
quinquina   55

ratafias   70, 71
Re, Filippo   91
Redi, Francesco   39, 49, 50–2,
    127, 151
  on birds' nests   56
  on 'Chiapa pepper'   54–5
  and chocolate   108, 109–10,
    110–11
  on *compotes*   67
  on ice combined with wine
    120–1
  on Italian parsimony   150
  on Morello cherries   119
  and stag's antlers   59–60, 61
  on viper meat   62, 63
'Reform cookery'   46
Regency years, and French
    cuisine   30, 37
Riccardi, Marquis Francesco   67
Ridolfi, Francesco   59
Risorgimento   34, 93, 96
Roberti, Count Giovan Battista
    13, 23, 27, 34, 37, 38, 96–9,
    144, 157
  on the bareness of tables   101

and *chacuterie*   155–6
on drinks   100
on the French   32–3
on the poverty of peasants
    96–7
on wine   89–90
on Zanzotti   139, 141–2
Robespierre, Maximilien Marie
    Isidore de   40
Roman Empire   132–3
Rome, pineapples in   86
Rome, ancient, use of fragrances
    66
rose water, disappearance of   5
rose-apples   84–5
roses   75–6
rosolios   70, 71
Rousseau, Jean-Jacques, *Emile*
    32

Sade, Donatien Alphonse
    François, Marquis de
    10–11
Saint-Evremond, Charles de
    38–9
Salvini, A. M.   43–4
Sanchez, Tommaso   59
Sanvitali, Count Jacopo   142
sauces   6
  French   139, 140
scents   84–7, 122–8
  Cardinal Moncada's perfumed
    Boveda   41–2
  changing tastes in   102–3
  of chocolate   110–11
  of roses   75
science, backlash of snobbery
    against   123
Semenzi, Father Giuseppe
    Girolamo   112, 113

sermons on noses   110
'service à la français'   67–8
sight, sense of
  food to appeal to the eye
    6–7, 106
  and gardens   95
  separation from taste   106
smells *see* scents
sorbets   70, 79, 85, 117, 130
  chocolate   72
Spain
  and chocolate   108
  decline in Spanish fashion   42
  Magalotti in   45
  and 'visual swigs'   119–20
spices
  disappearance of   5
  introduction of new   54–5
Spinoza, Baruch   14
stag antlers   59–60, 61
stairs   4
Stefani, Bartolomeo   33
strawberries   119
Strozzi, Father Tommaso   111, 112
Strozzi, Leone   77, 82, 83, 84
sturgeon   148
sugar   80, 157–60
Sulpicius Severus   150
Sydenham, Thomas   9
syrups   117

table liqueurs   70–1
table settings (*couverts*)   68
tables
  bareness of   101
  centre-of-table displays   68–9
tableware   68, 129
Talleyrand, Prince Charles-Maurice de   29

Tanara, Vincenzo   49
taste
  depravity in   11
  for elegance   34, 37, 38
  taverns, typical meals at   138
tea   55, 114, 117, 121, 130
  Bu tea   84
  green tea   84
Tenchin, Cardinal de   147
'terra japonica'/'terra catechu'   57
testicles, lambs'   77
Thousand and One Nights   147
tobacco   55, 118
Torricelli, Evangelista   80
Trivulzio, Prince Tolomeo   132
Tronchin (doctor to Voltaire)
  9–10
truffles   39, 40, 49
Turchi, Bishop Adeodato   22
turkey   49
Tuscany
  French customs and fashions
    67
  and pears   92

Utrecht, Treaty of   29

Vallisnieri, Antonio   109
vanilla   72, 73, 74
Vatel, Maître   28, 29
Vatican feasts   146–7
vegetables   48, 83, 93
  out of season   104
Verri, Alessandro   48, 65, 133–4, 140–1
Verri, Marquis Pietro   51, 132, 137, 156
  and chocolate   140–1
  on the French   1, 148, 149
  garden of   85

on the reform of food and
  cookery   46–8
on women at night   12–13
Vialardi, Giovanni   34
violet dinner   146–7
viper meat   60–3
'visual swigs'   119–20
Vitelli, Marquis Clemente   52
Vittorio Emanuele II, King of
  Italy   34
Voltaire, François Marie Arouet
  de   2, 8–10, 37, 86
  appearance   8–9

War of the Spanish Succession
  30
water, 'visual swigs' of   119–20
'water of cachou'   57
weekly pies   131
Winckelmann, Johann Joachim
  133–4, 135, 153
wine   79, 87–91
  foreign   20
  ice combined with   120–1
  snow-chilled   138

vipers drowned in   61, 62
watered down   47–8
Wolf, Friedrich August   3
women   101–5
  baroque   102
  effects of strong smells on
    64–5, 102–3
  and fans   19–20
  finery   21–2
  frivolous and elegant fashions
    100
  lack of appetite   101–2, 104–5
  lengthening and lightening of
    their figures   17
  and night life   12–13, 15
  spending long hours in bed
    100, 101
  suffering from convulsionary
    fits   9
  'toletta'   18–19
  and viper meat   60, 63

Zanotti, Francesco Maria   8, 88,
  141–2, 144
Zanotti, Giampietro   139, 144